The 50 Best

Oatmeal Cookies

in the World

Also by Honey and Larry Zisman

The 47 Best Chocolate Chip Cookies in the World
Super Sweets
The Great American Peanut Butter Book
The Great International Dessert Cookbook
The Burger Book
Chocolate Fantasies
The 55 Best Brownies in the World
The 50 Best Cheesecakes in the World

The 50 Best

Oatmeal Cookies

in the World

The Recipes That Won the
Nationwide "Ah! Oatmeal Cookies" Contest

Honey and Larry Zisman

ST. MARTIN'S PRESS ♦ NEW YORK

THE 50 BEST OATMEAL COOKIES IN THE WORLD. Copyright © 1994 by Honey and Larry Zisman. All rights reserved. Printed in the United States of America. No part of this book may be used or reproduced in any manner whatsoever without written permission except in the case of brief quotations embodied in critical articles or reviews. For information, address St. Martin's Press, 175 Fifth Avenue, New York, N.Y. 10010.

Library of Congress Cataloging-in-Publication Data

Zisman, Honey.
    The 50 best oatmeal cookies in the world / Honey and Larry Zisman.
        p.   cm.
    ISBN 0-312-10408-1
    1. Cookies.   2. Cookery (Oats)   3. Oatmeal.   I. Zisman, Larry.
    II. Title.   III. Title: Fifty best oatmeal cookies in the world.
    TX772.Z58   1994
    641.8′654—dc20   93-44022

10   9   8   7   6   5   4   3

for
SAMANTHA MICHAEL,
our favorite cookie rookie

OATMEAL COOKIES:

a BLAST from the past,
the WOW of now,
and
the BEST TO BE FED in the years ahead

Contents

An All-Time Favorite Just Gets Better and Better   1

Some Ideas and Suggestions about Cookie Baking   5

Some Oatmeal Cookies—Rich and Famous   11

The Award-Winning Recipes from the
  "Ah! Oatmeal Cookies" Contest   35

Index   141

An All-Time Favorite Just Gets Better and Better

With apologies to Will Rogers, it is quite truthful to say that just about everybody everywhere has never met an oatmeal cookie he or she didn't like.

There are good reasons for everybody everywhere to like oatmeal cookies. Just think of the benefits.

One, they are made from oatmeal, universally acclaimed as an all-natural, down-to-earth, good-for-you grain. Such food is a real treasure, especially cherished these days when it seems every day brings a new study showing that one more thing you never suspected will send you to an early grave.

Two, they are the perfect comfort food, bringing fond memories of childhood, coziness, hometowns, family, and real, old-time country and western music before city people started listening to it on the radio in their BMWs. Oatmeal is a state of mind.

Three, they are easy to make, even by people who are not sure they could tell the difference between an electric mixer and an electric chain saw.

And four, even if for some reason you are unable to bake your own oatmeal cookies and you are not living close enough to family and old friends to have some nice, fresh homemade oatmeal cookies made for you, they are available at every bakery, charity bakesale, farmers market . . . in fact, every place that offers honest, homey goodness.

Oatmeal cookies are really the best.

And now you are fortunate to have even more—the best of the best—the fifty winning recipes in the "Ah! Oatmeal Cookies" Contest, a friendly competition that attracted more than 5,000 recipes for oatmeal cookies of every kind imaginable.

Think about it. Here are the best oatmeal cookies out of more than 5,000 entries. You know that these winners are truly special since only one out of 100 was chosen as a winner.

But don't make a mistake and think that it was an easy or quick assignment to find these fifty winners. It was a long and difficult process that required baking and eating more oatmeal cookies than you . . . or anyone else . . . can imagine. But while it may have been difficult choosing the fifty best out of so many outstanding cookies, it was a job of pleasure, a task of fun, an endeavor with purpose.

And that purpose was to let everyone, everywhere enjoy the best oatmeal cookies possible.

So bake and eat these fifty winners, for they are certainly the best of the best. And remember: Whenever, wherever you eat an oatmeal cookie, you, too, will be a winner, even if you never entered the "Ah! Oatmeal Cookies" Contest.

Some Ideas and Suggestions about Cookie Baking

Although baking cookies is rather straightforward and uncomplicated compared to baking an elaborate French tart or doing your own taxes, it might still be helpful to consider several recommendations on the subject.

- Recipes are written on paper, not chiseled in stone. Accordingly, feel free to make substitutions in any cookie recipe that you are preparing. If the recipe calls for pecans and you like peanuts better, make the change. If the recipe says milk chocolate and you prefer semi-sweet, use what you like. If you are out of raspberry liqueur and the stores are closed at midnight on Wednesday when you are baking, use the apricot brandy that is already sitting on your shelf. Remember, you are the one who is making and eating the cookies, so use the ingredients you like best.
- Besides making substitutions in a recipe, also consider making additions if you desire. If you like nuts or pieces of fruit, feel free to add them even if the recipe does not mention them. Different flavorings—almond, mint, or vanilla—can be mixed into the batter according to your own tastes.
- To ensure that you have included all the ingredients in the proper order, there is an almost foolproof procedure to follow. Measure out all the ingredients and place them in individual containers in the appropriate order on the countertop before starting to mix them together. As you use each ingredient, remove its container. Then, if a container is gone, that means the ingredient has been added.
- You do not need a double boiler to melt chocolate or butter over hot water. Assemble the ingredients to be melted in an ordinary saucepan and place it in a larger pan containing hot or boiling water. This works just as well as a double boiler.

- You will get a more even blending of all the ingredients during mixing if you frequently scrape down the sides of the mixing bowl and the mixer blades.
- Chewy cookies or crispy cookies—that is the question. There is an ongoing, seemingly irreconcilable conflict between the partisans of each type of cookie. Since chewy cookies can be made crispy just by baking them a little longer, you can always bake half the cookie batter to be chewy and the other half a few minutes longer to be crispy. Everyone will be happy and satisfied. If only all the problems of the world could be solved so easily.
- The new insulated cookie sheets are quite good and help avoid burning the bottoms of the cookies.
- Since many ovens do not always bake at the exact temperature that is set on the dial, you might have to make adjustments in the cooking times called for in the recipes. As the time for the cookies to be done gets near, look inside the oven and see how well the cookies are baking and how much more time might be needed. For more exact baking, get and use an oven thermometer. They are inexpensive and can be purchased at any hardware or kitchen store.
- Some recipes call for the use of square baking pans to make bar cookies; most recipes use standard cookie sheets for roundish cookies. If you like one style better than the other, consider making bar cookies in a baking pan from a "round" cookie recipe, and vice versa. This change in baking procedure can be made easily, although it will require closely watching the cookies as they bake since the baking time specified for each version—baking pan versus cookie sheet—could differ and must be mod-

ified. Trial and error, along with close monitoring, will give you the correct baking time.

- Another change you might consider is to make one huge pizza pie–size cookie from a recipe instead of the usual standard-size cookies. These giant cookies are great decorated for parties, celebrations, and gifts.

- As you use different cookie recipes you will see instructions calling for greased or ungreased cookie sheets. Our experience has been that cookie sheets greased lightly with a little cooking oil spray yield the best results with just about every cookie.

- Cookies can easily be frozen by putting them in a tightly sealed plastic storage bag or container. It is best to defrost them while they are still in their container so they will not absorb excessive moisture. If you have time to prepare the cookie batter but not enough time to bake the cookies, the raw batter can be frozen in the same way as baked cookies. When you are ready to use the dough, however, the frozen raw batter should be defrosted in the refrigerator, still in its closed container, rather than on a countertop. After the batter is completely defrosted, it can be used to prepare and bake the cookies in the same way as using batter that has not been frozen and defrosted.

- Most of the cookies in this book are just cookies—simple and un-adorned—and they are quite good that way. But for something extra special, consider a variety of toppings even if not called for in the recipe. Some possibilities are melted chocolate drizzled over the top, a peanut butter and jelly mixture spread between two cookies to form a sandwich, and flaked coconut mixed into marshmallow fluff and spooned on top.

Your imagination and taste are the only limits to dressing up whatever cookies you make.

- Everyone has seen decorated cakes for birthdays, anniversaries, and other special occasions. Why not have decorated cookies instead of a cake for a change? The same themes and kinds of decorations that are used for cakes can be applied to cookies but, of course, on a smaller scale.
- It is quite customary to bring a bottle of wine or a bunch of flowers as a gift when going to someone's home as a guest for dinner. How about bringing a batch of homemade cookies instead? Everyone likes cookies, and giving a homemade gift is always more thoughtful and in good taste . . . and tastes good!
- Knowing how to cook and bake is a valuable skill for everyone, regardless of gender or marital status. Cooking and baking can also be quite rewarding careers or hobbies. Since cookie-baking is a relatively easy and safe activity in the kitchen, you can start your children baking cookies at an early age. Cookie-making has a variety of operations requiring only minimal skills and a fairly wide latitude of exactness, so it is a great introduction to baking for a very young person. And, if by some chance the cookies do not come out exactly right, it is only a small investment in time and money that will have been lost.

Some Oatmeal Cookies—Rich and Famous

• OATMEAL COOKIE BITES •

from Willard Scott

½ cup sugar
1 egg, beaten
1 teaspoon shortening, melted
½ teaspoon vanilla
½ cup uncooked rolled oats

½ cup chopped nuts
¼ teaspoon salt
1 tablespoon honey
raisins (optional)

1. Preheat oven to 375° F.
2. Gradually add sugar to beaten egg. Mix in melted shortening and vanilla. Stir in oats, nuts, salt, and honey, blending well. (Sometimes we add raisins to the batter, too.)
3. Drop by teaspoonfuls onto greased cookie sheets and press with fork.
4. Bake for 10 to 12 minutes.

Yield: approximately 2 dozen cookies

In Europe, up until about 1900 only horses and peasants ate oats because they were cheap and plentiful. The rich were able to afford wheat bread, which had a baked golden-brown crust on top. Thus, the elite of society became known as the "upper crust" because of the bread they ate.

· OATMEAL COOKIES ·

by Bill Blass

¾ cup unsalted butter
1 cup firmly packed brown sugar
½ cup sugar
1 egg
¼ cup water
1 teaspoon vanilla
3 cups uncooked quick rolled oats
1 cup raisins

1 cup chopped walnuts
1 teaspoon salt
1 cup all-purpose flour
½ teaspoon baking soda
1 teaspoon cinnamon
½ teaspoon ground cloves
½ teaspoon ground ginger
¼ teaspoon nutmeg

1. Preheat oven to 350° F.
2. Cream together butter, brown sugar, and sugar. Add egg, water, and vanilla, beating until light. Add oats, raisins, walnuts, salt, flour, baking soda, cinnamon, cloves, ginger, and nutmeg, mixing together thoroughly.
3. Drop by teaspoonfuls onto lightly greased cookie sheets.
4. Bake for 12 to 15 minutes.

Yield: approximately 6 dozen cookies

◆ SALLY'S OATMEAL COOKIES ◆

from Sally Jessy Raphael

3 cups sifted flour
1 teaspoon baking soda
1 teaspoon salt
1 teaspoon cinnamon
3 cups uncooked rolled oats
1 cup sugar

1 cup dark brown sugar, firmly
   packed
1 cup raisins
1 cup vegetable oil
2 eggs
⅓ cup milk

1. Preheat oven to 375° F.

2. Sift flour, baking soda, salt, and cinnamon together into a very large mixing bowl. Set aside.

3. Combine oats, sugar, brown sugar, raisins, vegetable oil, eggs, and milk, mixing together well. Stir in flour mixture.

4. Drop by rounded tablespoonfuls, the size of walnuts, onto cookie sheets lined with foil.

5. Bake for 15 to 20 minutes on the center rack, reversing the cookie sheets once halfway through the cooking period. If the cookie bottoms are burning, place another cookie sheet under each one of the original cookie sheets and try baking one cookie sheet at a time.

6. Remove from oven and let cool on a wire rack. Cookies can be frozen or stored in an airtight container.

Yield: approximately 4 dozen cookies

Unless you have been isolated on the moon for the last ten years you know that oats are extremely nutritious, and that eating them will help reduce cholesterol levels in the blood. But there is much more. Oats are high in water-soluble fiber, which makes them ideal for people who want to lose weight since oats absorb water, giving you a feeling of fullness. In addition, oats contain B vitamins, Vitamin A, Vitamin E, thiamine, riboflavin, folic acid, iron, and calcium. And, finally, oats are low in fat and high in protein—even higher than wheat.

• OAT BISCUITS •

from Vidal and Ronnie Sassoon

3 tablespoons margarine
5 tablespoons lard
⅓ cup casher (unbleached natural)
    sugar

½ egg
few drops vanilla
⅞ cup self-rising flour
uncooked rolled oats

1. Preheat oven to 375° F.
2. Cream together margarine, lard, and sugar until light and fluffy. Mix in egg, vanilla, and flour, blending well.
3. Using wet hands, roll batter into small balls and coat with rolled oats.
4. Place on greased and floured cookie sheets, allowing room for cookies to spread, and press out slightly with hands.
5. Bake for 20 minutes. Remove from cookie sheets and cool on wire rack.

Yield: approximately 2 dozen cookies

Per capita consumption of oats in the United States is about 3 pounds a year.

• OATMEAL CRISPS •

A favorite of Jack and Barbara Nicklaus

¼ cup butter
¾ cup shortening
1 cup light brown sugar
1 egg, beaten
1 teaspoon vanilla

1½ cups all-purpose flour
½ teaspoon baking soda
½ teaspoon baking powder
dash salt
1¼ cups uncooked quick rolled oats
1 cup flaked coconut

1. Preheat oven to 375° F.
2. Cream together butter and shortening. Add sugar, egg, and vanilla, mixing together well. Sift together flour, baking soda, baking powder, and salt and then gradually add to creamed mixture. Stir in oats and coconut.
3. Drop by teaspoonfuls onto cookie sheets and press with fork.
4. Bake for 12 to 15 minutes.

Yield: approximately 4 dozen cookies

William Tryon was an English shepherd, a successful businessman in Barbados and London, and, later in life, a philosopher devoted to pursuing (and encouraging others to pursue) a healthy life.

Tryon recommended vegetarianism, cleanliness, abstinence from tobacco and alcohol, silent meditation, mysticism, and avoidance of extravagance. His best-known writings were contained in *Way to Health*, published in 1683. This book greatly impressed and influenced Benjamin Franklin, who read it as a youth . . . but obviously did not follow its advice later in life.

Of more interest to oatmeal lovers is that in *Way to Health*, Tryon wrote that "Oatmeal is to be accounted the best of all Flour."

• OATMEAL ICEBOX COOKIES •

from Billy Graham

1 cup brown sugar	*1 teaspoon baking soda*
1 cup sugar	*1 teaspoon salt*
1 cup margarine, softened	*1 teaspoon vanilla*
2 eggs	*3 cups uncooked rolled oats*
1 cup flour	*2 cups nuts, chopped*

1. Cream together brown sugar, sugar, and margarine. Add eggs, mixing well. Sift together flour, baking soda, and salt and add to creamed mixture. Mix in vanilla, oats, and nuts.

2. On a floured surface, roll batter into several long rolls and wrap each roll in wax paper. Store in freezer until needed.

3. To bake cookies, preheat oven to 300° F.

4. Cut rolls into thin slices and place cookies well-spaced on greased cookie sheets.

5. Bake for 10 to 15 minutes.

Yield: approximately 6 dozen cookies

The May 1993 issue of *Consumer Reports* magazine contains an article about new, healthy versions of foods available in the supermarket. The magazine chose four popular foods to test as representative samples of what people like to eat. The four types of food were American cheese, mayonnaise, salad dressing, and, of course, oatmeal-raisin cookies.

• ANZAC BISCUITS •

from Paul Keating, Prime Minister of Australia

1 cup rolled oats
1 cup flour
1 cup sugar
¾ cup flaked coconut

½ cup butter
2 tablespoons pancake syrup
½ teaspoon baking soda
1 tablespoon boiling water

1. Preheat oven to 350° F.
2. Combine oats, flour, sugar, and coconut. Set aside.
3. Combine butter and pancake syrup and cook over low heat until melted. Set aside.
4. Mix together baking soda and water and add to butter mixture. Mix into oat mixture.
5. Place tablespoons of batter onto lightly greased cookie sheets about 2 inches apart.
6. Bake for about 20 minutes.
7. Loosen cookies from cookie sheets while still warm and then let cool on sheets.

Yield: approximately 3 dozen cookies

• QUAKER'S BEST OATMEAL COOKIES •

1¼ cups margarine, softened
¾ cup firmly packed brown sugar
½ cup sugar
1 egg
1 teaspoon vanilla
1½ cups all-purpose flour

1 teaspoon baking soda
½ teaspoon salt (optional)
1 teaspoon cinnamon
¼ teaspoon nutmeg
3 cups QUAKER Oats (quick or old-fashioned, uncooked)

1. Preheat oven to 375° F.

2. Beat together margarine, brown sugar, and sugar until creamy. Beat in egg and vanilla. Set aside.

3. Combine flour, baking soda, salt, cinnamon, and nutmeg. Mix into sugar mixture. Stir in oats.

4. Drop by rounded tablespoonfuls onto ungreased cookie sheets.

5. Bake for 8 to 9 minutes for chewy cookies or 10 to 11 minutes for crispy cookies.

6. Cool for 1 minute on cookie sheets and then remove to wire rack.

Yield: approximately 4½ dozen cookies

To make bar cookies, press batter onto the bottom of an ungreased 9-inch by 13-inch pan.

Bake at 375° F for about 25 minutes, until light golden brown.

Let cool completely and then cut into 1½-inch squares.

Yield: approximately 4 dozen bars

Variations:

If desired, add any one or a combination of any two of the following ingredients:

1 cup raisins
1 cup chopped nuts
1 cup semi-sweet chocolate chips

1 cup butterscotch chips
1 cup peanut butter–flavored chips

Nutrition information for 1 cookie:
　　Calories—90
　　Calories from fat—45
　　Total fat—5g
　　Saturated fat—1g
　　Cholesterol—5mg
　　Sodium—70mg
　　Total carbohydrates—11g
　　Dietary fiber—0g
　　Protein—1g

Courtesy of The Quaker Oats Company

· JUMBO OAT COOKIES ·

¾ cup sugar
⅓ cup margarine, softened
⅓ cup light corn syrup
2 egg whites, slightly beaten
1 teaspoon almond extract
2¼ cups QUAKER Oats (quick or
  old-fashioned, uncooked)

1 cup all-purpose flour
½ teaspoon baking soda
½ teaspoon salt (optional)
3 tablespoons sliced almonds

1. Preheat oven to 350° F.

2. Beat together sugar, margarine, and corn syrup until fluffy. Add egg whites and almond extract, mixing well. Set aside.

3. Combine oats, flour, baking soda, salt, and almonds. Mix into sugar mixture.

4. Drop by ¼-measuring cupfuls onto ungreased cookie sheets about 2 inches apart. Press with fingertips into 3-inch circles.

5. Bake for 14 to 16 minutes or until light golden brown.

6. Cool for 1 minute on cookie sheets. Remove to aluminum foil and let cool completely.

7. Store in a tightly covered container.

Yield: approximately 1 dozen cookies

Nutrition information for 1 cookie:
  Calories—230

Calories from fat—63
Total fat—7g
Cholesterol—0mg
Sodium—110mg
Total carbohydrates—38g
Dietary fiber—2g
Protein—4g

Courtesy of The Quaker Oats Company

• CHOC-OAT-CHIP COOKIES •

1 cup margarine or butter, softened
1¼ cups firmly packed brown sugar
½ cup sugar
2 eggs
2 tablespoons milk
2 teaspoons vanilla
1¾ cups all-purpose flour
1 teaspoon baking soda

½ teaspoon salt (optional)
2½ cups QUAKER Oats (quick or
 old-fashioned, uncooked)
1 12-ounce package (2 cups)
 NESTLÉ TOLL HOUSE Semi-
 Sweet Chocolate Morsels
1 cup coarsely chopped nuts (optional)

1. Preheat oven to 375° F.

2. Beat together margarine, brown sugar, and sugar until creamy. Add eggs, milk, and vanilla, beating well. Add flour, baking soda and salt, mixing well. Stir in oats, chocolate morsels, and nuts, mixing well.

3. Drop by rounded tablespoonfuls onto ungreased cookie sheets.

4. Bake for 9 to 10 minutes for chewy cookies or 12 to 13 minutes for crispy cookies.

5. Cool for 1 minute on cookie sheets. Remove to wire racks and let cool completely.

For Raisin Spice Oatmeal Cookies, prepare as described above but add 1 teaspoon cinnamon and ¼ teaspoon nutmeg and substitute 1 cup raisins for the chocolate morsels.

Yield: approximately 5 dozen cookies

To make Easy Bar Cookies, press batter onto bottom of an ungreased 9-inch by 13-inch pan.

Bake at 375° F for 35 to 40 minutes or until light golden brown.

Let cool completely and then cut into bars.

Yield: approximately 3 dozen bars

Nutrition information for 1 cookie:
   Calories—110
   Calories from fat—45
   Total fat—5g
   Saturated fat—1g
   Cholesterol—5mg
   Sodium—50mg
   Total carbohydrates—15g
   Dietary fiber—0g
   Protein—1g

Courtesy of The Quaker Oats Company

◆ JOHN McCANN'S IRISH OATMEAL COOKIES ◆

McCann's Irish Oatmeal
Naas, County Kildare, Ireland

1¼ cups margarine
½ cup firmly packed brown sugar
½ cup sugar
1 egg, slightly beaten
1 teaspoon vanilla
1½ cups all-purpose flour
1 teaspoon baking soda

1 teaspoon salt (optional)
1 teaspoon cinnamon (optional)
3 cups uncooked McCann's Quick
   Cooking Oatmeal
¾ cup raisins
½ cup walnuts

1. Preheat oven to 375° F.
2. Cream together margarine, brown sugar, and sugar. Add egg and vanilla. Set aside.
3. Stir together flour, baking soda, salt, and cinnamon, and add to shortening mixture. Mix well. Stir in oats, raisins, and walnuts.
4. Drop rounded teaspoonfuls of batter onto an ungreased cookie sheet.
5. Bake 12 to 15 minutes. Cool 1 minute before removing to wire cooling rack.

Yield: 4½ dozen cookies

The Pilgrims who came to America on the *Mayflower* in 1620 to establish a colony in present-day Massachusetts brought a supply of oats with them.

• NANTUCKET BAKE SHOP OATMEAL COOKIES •

Nantucket Island, Massachusetts

3½ cups brown sugar
½ cup plus 2 tablespoons
  shortening
½ cup plus 2 tablespoons
  margarine
1 tablespoon plus 2 teaspoons
  baking soda
1 teaspoon vanilla

1 tablespoon cinnamon
3 eggs
3 cups flour
3½ cups uncooked rolled oats
1¼ cups raisins, soaked in water

1. Preheat oven to 375° F.

2. Cream together sugar, shortening, margarine, baking soda, vanilla, and cinnamon. Mix until smooth. Add eggs. Mix, scrape bowl, and mix again. Add flour and mix. Add oats and mix for 5 minutes. Drain raisins and add to batter. (An electric mixer is recommended for all mixing.)

3. Drop by tablespoonfuls onto greased or papered cookie sheets.

4. Bake for 15 to 18 minutes, depending on whether you want chewy or crispy cookies.

Yield: approximately 5 dozen cookies

• PENNY'S PASTRIES •

Austin, Texas

1 cup vegetable shortening	*1 teaspoon salt*
1 cup brown sugar	*1 teaspoon baking soda*
1 cup sugar	*1 teaspoon cinnamon*
2 eggs	*2 cups uncooked rolled oats*
2 teaspoons vanilla	*1 cup pecans, chopped*
1½ cups flour	*1 cup chopped dates or raisins*

1. Preheat oven to 350° F.
2. Cream together shortening, brown sugar, and sugar. Add eggs and vanilla. Set aside.
3. Mix together flour, salt, baking soda, and cinnamon in a small bowl. Add flour mixture to cream mixture. Add oats and mix well. Stir in nuts and dates or raisins.
4. Drop by teaspoonfuls onto a parchment-lined cookie sheet.
5. Bake for 10 minutes.

Yield: approximately 6 dozen cookies

Mention eating out in New York City and most people immediately think of expensive French restaurants, exotic foreign cuisines, trendy celebrity gathering spots, and formal hotel dining rooms. But in an article about oatmeal in *The New York Times*, it is noted that "New York is full of restaurants and diners that serve good, nourishing versions of oatmeal."

As they say, if you can't get it in New York, you can't get it anywhere.

The Award-Winning Recipes from the "Ah! Oatmeal Cookies" Contest

• GUM DROP COOKIES •

Sister Martha Schuler
Livermore, Kentucky

1 cup shortening
1 cup sugar
1 cup brown sugar
2 eggs
1 teaspoon vanilla
2 cups flour
1 teaspoon baking powder

1 teaspoon baking soda
½ teaspoon salt
2 cups uncooked rolled oats
1 cup coconut
1 cup gum drops, finely cut
½ cup black walnuts

1. Preheat oven to 350° F.
2. Cream together shortening, sugar, and brown sugar. Add in eggs and vanilla, mixing well. Blend in flour, baking powder, baking soda, salt, rolled oats, coconut, gum drops, and walnuts.
3. Roll into 1-inch-diameter balls and place on greased cookie sheets, pressing down with a fork.
4. Bake for 10 minutes.

Yield: approximately 5 dozen cookies

• FROSTED ORANGE DROPS •

Margaret Pittorf
Amherst, New York

2 cups flour
½ teaspoon baking soda
½ teaspoon salt
2 cups uncooked quick rolled oats
1 cup butter or margarine
1 cup sugar

2 eggs
1 teaspoon vanilla
½ cup orange marmalade
Frosting (recipe follows)
walnut halves

1. Preheat oven to 350° F.
2. Sift together flour, baking soda, and salt. Stir in oats. Set aside.
3. Cream together butter, add sugar gradually, creaming well. Add eggs and vanilla, beating until light and fluffy. Blend in flour mixture and marmalade.
4. Drop by rounded tablespoonfuls onto greased cookie sheets.
5. Bake for 12 to 15 minutes, until light brown. Remove from oven and let cool.
6. Spread Frosting over center of each cookie and then top with a walnut half.

Yield: approximately 4 dozen cookies

FROSTING

⅓ cup butter or margarine
3 cups confectioners' sugar
milk

Melt and lightly brown butter. Stir in confectioners' sugar and add just enough milk to make a good spreading consistency.

· CHOCOLATE-ALMOND DELIGHTS ·

Betty J. Nichols
Eugene, Oregon

1 cup flour
1 teaspoon baking powder
½ teaspoon salt
½ cup butter or margarine
1 cup sugar
1 egg
2 ounces unsweetened chocolate, melted

1 teaspoon vanilla
1 teaspoon almond extract
1 cup uncooked rolled oats, quick or old-fashioned
⅔ cup sliced almonds, coarsely chopped

1. Preheat oven to 350° F.
2. Sift together flour, baking powder, and salt. Set aside.
3. Cream together butter and sugar until well blended. Beat in egg, melted chocolate, vanilla, and almond extract. Stir in flour mixture, oats, and almonds.
4. Drop by teaspoonfuls onto lightly greased cookie sheets and flatten with a knife or spatula dipped in cold water.
5. Bake for 8 to 10 minutes, until light brown. Remove cookies from cookie sheets and let cool on wire rack.

Yield: approximately 5 dozen cookies

In Scotland "we cultivate literature on a little oatmeal."
                    —Sydney Smith (clergyman, essayist, and
                              editor who lived from 1771 to 1845)

· SOUTHERN OATMEAL BARS ·

Andrea Wexstten
Herrin, Illinois

½ cup butter or margarine
½ cup firmly packed brown sugar
½ teaspoon vanilla
1 cup uncooked quick rolled oats
¾ cup flour

2 tablespoons wheat germ
¼ teaspoon salt
¼ teaspoon baking soda
1 cup nuts, finely chopped
Filling (recipe follows)

1. Preheat oven to 350° F.
2. Cream together butter, brown sugar, and vanilla. Beat until fluffy. Set aside.
3. Mix together oats, flour, wheat germ, salt, and baking soda. Stir into butter mixture. Batter will be crumbly.
4. Pat three-quarters of the batter onto the bottom of a lightly greased 9-inch square pan.
5. Bake for 10 minutes. Remove from oven and let cool while making Filling.
6. Pour Filling over baked crust and set aside. Combine nuts and remaining batter and sprinkle over Filling.

7. Return to oven and bake at 350° F for 25 to 30 minutes more. Remove from oven and let cool. Cut into bars about 1½ inches by 2 inches.

Yield: approximately 2½ dozen bars

FILLING

1 egg, slightly beaten
1 cup mashed cooked sweet
  potatoes

⅔ cup sweetened condensed milk
1 teaspoon pumpkin pie spice
½ teaspoon orange peel

Combine all ingredients and mix together well.

What's Cookin' is a health-food restaurant on East 41st Street in Manhattan. Every morning during the cold winter months the restaurant serves about 200 bowls of oatmeal to a broad range of customers dressed in a complete range of attire from construction overalls to three-piece suits.

According to Sharon Ben-Mayer, the thirty-six-year-old owner and chef (she is also a nutritionist), "The secret is, I add a little honey, but not too much. Just enough so that you don't have to add any sugar." She also adds some whole milk and farina but no salt.

The oatmeal at What's Cookin' is described as "creamy smooth."

• RHUBARB-OAT BARS •

Noreen Loomans Burton
Racine, Wisconsin

1½ cups uncooked rolled oats
1 cup light brown sugar
1 cup margarine
1½ cups flour
½ teaspoon baking soda
½ cup chopped nuts
Rhubarb Filling (recipe follows)

1. Preheat oven to 350° F.
2. Stir together oats, brown sugar, margarine, flour, baking soda, and nuts, mixing until crumbly.
3. Pat three-quarters of the mixture onto the bottom and slightly up the sides of a greased 9-inch by 13-inch pan. Make sure that mixture covers pan completely, leaving no holes.
4. Spread hot Rhubarb Filling evenly on crust, leaving about ¼ inch of crust uncovered around edges.
5. Sprinkle remaining one-quarter of crumbly mixture over Rhubarb Filling. Topping should be dry and easy to sprinkle. If it clumps, mix in a small amount of flour so it will sprinkle evenly.
6. Bake for 30 minutes. Remove from oven, let cool, and then cut into 1-inch by 2-inch bars.

Yield: approximately 4 dozen bars

Rhubarb Filling

1½ cups sugar
2 tablespoons cornstarch
3 cups thinly sliced fresh or frozen
   rhubarb

¼ cup water (only if fresh rhubarb is
   used)
1 teaspoon vanilla

1. Mix together sugar and cornstarch until smooth. Set aside.
2. Put rhubarb, water (if used), vanilla, and sugar mixture in a heavy saucepan and cook over medium heat until thick.

The ancient Romans were the first to domesticate oats when they started planting it as a crop around 2500 B.C. They had discovered that oats were edible and started planting it to be grown for food.

• CREAM CHEESE OATMEAL SANDWICHES •

Betty S. Gregory
Greensboro, North Carolina

½ cup margarine
2 cups firmly packed light brown
  sugar
2 eggs
2 cups flour
2 teaspoons baking soda

2 cups uncooked quick rolled oats
2 teaspoons cinnamon
1 tablespoon vanilla
½ cup chopped nuts
½ cup raisins
Filling (recipe follows)

1. Preheat oven to 350° F.
2. Cream together margarine and brown sugar. Beat in eggs. Set aside.
3. Stir together flour and baking soda. Add oats and cinnamon. Mix into cream mixture. Stir in vanilla, nuts, and raisins.
4. Drop by teaspoonfuls 2 inches apart onto greased cookie sheets. Flatten with the bottom of a glass.
5. Bake for 10 minutes. Remove cookies from cookie sheets and let cool on a wire rack.
6. Spread Filling on the flat side of a cookie and top with another cookie to form a sandwich.

Yield: approximately 3 dozen sandwich cookies

FILLING

4 ounces cream cheese, softened
½ cup margarine, melted

1 teaspoon vanilla
3¾ cups confectioners' sugar

Cream together cream cheese, margarine, vanilla, and confectioners' sugar.

The final scene in the Academy Award–winning movie *Moonstruck* takes place with everyone sitting around the table in the Castorini family kitchen in Brooklyn.

And what a scene it is!

There is Loretta (played by Cher), a widow in her thirties who is in love with her fiancé's brother; Cher's parents, Cosmo and Rose (who just told her husband to stop seeing his mistress), played by Vincent Gardenia and Olympia Dukakis; and Ronny Cammareri (Nicolas Cage), the moody but volatile baker who was going to be Cher's future brother-in-law until they met and went to the opera together. Everyone is waiting for the arrival of Johnny Cammareri (Danny Aiello), Cher's fiancé and Ronny's brother, who just got back to the United States after visiting his supposedly dying mother in Italy.

The air, as the cliché says, is so thick you could cut it with a knife. But what was it that kept everyone civil, stable, and steady in such a situation?

Oatmeal!

Rose Castorini had the good sense to give everyone a bowl of hot oatmeal as they came together for what in another time or in another movie would have been a gunfight at the OK Corral. But not in Brooklyn, where on that day everything worked out all right.

• APPLE OATMEAL BREAKFAST COOKIES •

Lois L. Shaffer
Jay, Maine

1½ cups uncooked quick rolled oats
¼ cup whole wheat flour
½ cup chopped dates
½ teaspoon salt

¼ cup chopped walnuts
¼ cup orange juice
1½ cups shredded apple

1. Preheat oven to 375° F.
2. Combine oats, flour, dates, salt, walnuts, orange juice, and shredded apple. Let stand for 10 minutes.
3. Drop by large tablespoonfuls 2 inches apart onto cookie sheets coated with cooking spray.
4. Bake for 18 to 22 minutes, until light brown.

Yield: approximately 2½ dozen large cookies

• CHOCOLATE MINT DIPPERS •

Janice Murray
Boston, Massachusetts

¾ cup brown sugar
¼ cup sugar
½ cup margarine
½ cup shortening
1 egg
1 teaspoon chocolate mint liqueur
1⅓ cups flour

1 teaspoon baking soda
1 teaspoon baking powder
dash salt
1 cup flaked coconut
1½ cups uncooked rolled oats
Chocolate Mint Dip (recipe follows)

1. Preheat oven to 375° F.
2. Cream together brown sugar, sugar, margarine, and shortening. Mix in egg and liqueur. Set aside.
3. Sift together flour, baking soda, baking powder, and salt. Mix into cream mixture. Stir in coconut and oats.
4. Drop by teaspoonfuls onto greased cookie sheets.
5. Bake for 13 to 15 minutes, until lightly browned. Let cool slightly. Remove cookies from cookie sheets and cool completely on wire rack.
6. Holding cookies with thumb and two fingers, dunk into hot Chocolate

Mint Dip, covering about three-quarters of the cookie. Place dipped cookies on a tray covered with wax paper and refrigerate until chocolate coating is hard.

Yield: approximately 5 dozen cookies

CHOCOLATE MINT DIP

1¼ pounds mint chocolate
5 ounces unsweetened chocolate

½ cup plus 2 tablespoons margarine
5 tablespoons chocolate mint liqueur

Place mint chocolate, unsweetened chocolate, and margarine in a heavy saucepan and heat over hot water, stirring occasionally, until melted. Remove from heat and stir in liqueur.

More oatmeal is eaten in New York City—almost 16 million pounds a year—than in any other city in the United States.

• YUM RUM COOKIES •

Cathie Davis
Yacolt, Washington

½ cup sugar
½ cup brown sugar
½ cup butter
½ cup shortening
1 egg
1½ cups uncooked quick rolled oats
1 cup flaked coconut
1½ cups flour

1 teaspoon baking soda
1 teaspoon vanilla
¼ teaspoon salt
3 tablespoons rum, brandy, or sherry wine
walnut halves, pecan halves, or maraschino cherries (optional)

1. Preheat oven to 375° F.

2. Cream together sugar, brown sugar, butter, and shortening. Add egg, oats, and coconut, mixing together well. Set aside.

3. Sift together flour and baking soda. Combine with cream mixture. Stir in vanilla, salt, and rum.

4. Drop by teaspoonfuls onto greased cookie sheets. Make an indentation across the top of each cookie with a fork that has been dipped in flour. If desired, top cookies with walnut halves, pecan halves, or maraschino cherries.

5. Bake for 8 to 9 minutes for chewy cookies or 10 to 11 minutes for crispy cookies. Let cool slightly on cookie sheets and then remove to wire racks.

Yield: approximately 4½ dozen cookies

Is there such a thing as a miracle product? The people at Nurture, Inc., in Missoula, Montana, could be excused if they answer "Yes."

The company produces a product called, not surprisingly, Nurture, which is made from oats and does an amazing variety of things. Nurture acts as a sponge that can absorb any type of water-based or oil-based substance and then release it gradually. The applications of Nurture are quite varied and include cosmetics, oil spill remedies, food preservatives, sunscreens, pesticides, and dermatological drugs.

And oats make good cookies, too.

In a cheap shot at the Scottish people, Dr. Samuel Johnson, in his *Dictionary of the English Language*, written in 1755, defined oats as "a grain which is generally given to horses, but in Scotland supports the people."

Patrick Murray, a Scottish politician and writer and the fifth Lord Elibank, responded to Mr. Johnson's unkind remark with the retort, "Very true, and where else will you find such horses and such men?"

• OATMEAL PLUS-PLUS COOKIES •

Pat Rush Benigno
Ridgeland, Mississippi

1 cup butter or margarine, softened
1 cup sugar
1 cup firmly packed brown sugar
2 eggs, lightly beaten
½ teaspoon vanilla
1¼ cups all-purpose flour

1 teaspoon baking soda
½ teaspoon salt
3 cups uncooked rolled oats
1 cup chopped macadamia nuts
1 cup white chocolate chunks

1. Preheat oven to 350° F.
2. Cream together butter, sugar, brown sugar, eggs, and vanilla. Set aside.
3. Mix together flour, baking soda, and salt. Stir in oats, macadamia nuts, and white chocolate chunks.
4. Shape batter into 1-inch-diameter balls and place on lightly greased cookie sheets.
5. Bake for 11 to 13 minutes.

Yield: approximately 8 dozen cookies

The anti-itch and anti-irritant properties of whole oat grain have been known since ancient times. It's no surprise, then, that oats are commonly used today in specialty soaps and facial masks.

• GERRY'S MOLASSES COOKIES •

Gerry Poynton
Buffalo, New York

1¾ cups flour	2 eggs
1 teaspoon baking powder	½ cup shortening
1 teaspoon baking soda	6 tablespoons molasses
½ teaspoon salt	1 teaspoon vanilla
1¼ cups sugar	2 cups rolled oats

1. Preheat oven to 350° F.
2. Sift together flour, baking powder, baking soda, and salt. Mix in sugar, eggs, shortening, molasses, and vanilla. Stir until smooth. Fold in oats. Batter will be very stiff.
3. Drop by heaping teaspoonfuls onto greased cookie sheets.
4. Bake for 12 to 15 minutes.

Yield: approximately 3 dozen cookies

• APRICOT-OAT THUMBPRINTS •

Sylvia Richard
Goffstown, New Hampshire

1 cup confectioners' sugar
¾ cup vegetable shortening
¼ cup orange juice
2 tablespoons vanilla
1½ cups all-purpose flour

1½ cups uncooked rolled oats
dash salt
½ cup apricot jam
Drizzle Topping (recipe follows)

1. Preheat oven to 350° F.
2. Using an electric mixer, beat confectioners' sugar and shortening until light and fluffy. Beat in orange juice and vanilla until well blended. Set aside.
3. Combine flour, oats, and salt. Beat into sugar mixture.
4. Drop by tablespoonfuls 1 inch apart onto greased cookie sheets. Press lightly in middle of each cookie and place about 1 teaspoon of apricot jam in each hole.
5. Bake for 18 to 20 minutes, until lightly browned. Remove from oven and let cool.
6. Decorate each cookie with Drizzle Topping.

Yield: approximately 2 dozen cookies

DRIZZLE TOPPING

¼ cup confectioners' sugar   *1 tablespoon milk*

Stir together confectioners' sugar and milk.

For many children, having oatmeal for breakfast was a familiar and important part of growing up. But for some children, oatmeal was truly a foreign experience.

Among the many exhibits of artifacts, documents, and photographs displayed in the Ellis Island Immigration Museum in New York City, there are numerous quotes from interviews with people who were processed at Ellis Island when they arrived in America from Europe many years ago.

Consider the following quote from an interview that took place in 1985 with Oreste Teglia, who was a young immigrant from Italy when she passed through Ellis Island in 1916:

> We got oatmeal for breakfast. I didn't know what it was, with brown sugar on it you know. I couldn't get myself to eat it. So I put it on the windowsill, let the birds eat it.

It would not be unreasonable to assume that the Americanization of Oreste Teglia included many, many bowls of oatmeal since 1916, and that she not only learned to recognize it, but also came to look forward to enjoying her hot cereal every cold, winter morning.

The countries that grow the most oats are the United States, Russia, Canada, France, and Germany. The American states that produce the most oats are South Dakota (number one), followed in turn by North Dakota, Wisconsin, Minnesota, and Iowa.

• PEPPERMINT TOPPERS •

Flo Burtnett
Gage, Oklahoma

1 cup margarine
1 cup brown sugar
1 egg
2 cups flour
1 teaspoon baking soda

½ teaspoon salt
2 cups uncooked quick rolled oats
½ cup plus 3 tablespoons crushed
    peppermint candy
Glaze (recipe follows)

1. Preheat oven to 375° F.
2. Cream together margarine and brown sugar until light and fluffy. Blend in egg. Set aside.
3. Sift together flour, baking soda, and salt. Add to cream mixture. Stir in oats and ½ cup of the peppermint candy, mixing well.
4. Roll into 1-inch-diameter balls and place about 2 inches apart on greased cookie sheets.
5. Bake for 10 to 12 minutes. Remove from oven, let cool for 1 minute, and then remove cookies to wire racks to cool completely.
6. Drizzle Glaze over cookies. Sprinkle remaining 3 tablespoons of crushed peppermint candy over top.

Yield: approximately 4 dozen cookies

GLAZE

1½ cups sifted confectioners' sugar   *3 tablespoons milk*

Combine confectioners' sugar and milk, mixing together well.

Linguistically speaking, oats are treated differently from the other common grains. Oats have a plural form with an *s* but wheat, rye, barley, maize, corn, rice, and millet all have no separate plural word.

The city slicker looking at the farmer's field might say, "Wow, look at all those oats" but he would never say "Wow, look at all those wheats." Using such exclamations as examples assumes, of course, that a city slicker could tell the difference between oats and wheat without reading it on the wrapper from a loaf of bread.

• BUTTERSCOTCH NO-BAKES •

May McClelland
Hudson, Florida

2 cups sugar
¾ cup butter or margarine
⅔ cup evaporated milk
1 3¼-ounce package instant or
  regular butterscotch pudding

3½ cups uncooked quick rolled oats
1 teaspoon vanilla
¾ cup nuts

1. In a large heavy saucepan, combine sugar, butter, and milk. Heat to a rolling boil, stirring frequently.

2. Remove from heat and add butterscotch pudding and oats. Stir in vanilla and nuts. Let cool for 15 minutes.

3. Drop by rounded teaspoonfuls onto wax paper. Let cool completely.

Yield: approximately 5 dozen cookies

Oatmeal is good for you—not just inside your body but outside as well.

In one episode of the popular television series "Northern Exposure," set in the fictitious town of Cicely, Alaska, the residents are set upon by the annual swarms of mosquitoes.

Most of the residents are used to this yearly plague. But for Joel Fleischman, the very homesick town doctor who has reluctantly moved to Cicely from New York City in order to meet his medical school obligations, the attacks of these nasty little insects are most distressing. So how does Dr. Fleischman find relief?

Relief comes to him from a nice colloidal oatmeal bath that, as the doctor explains, neutralizes the pH level of the skin to stop the itching . . . as well as from a compassionate back-scratching from his ever-bickering friend Maggie O'Connell.

· EASY-BREEZY BLUEBERRY TREATS ·

Crystal Morein
Lake Charles, Louisiana

1 13- or 14-ounce blueberry muffin
  mix package with separate tin of
  blueberries included
¾ cup uncooked quick rolled oats

¼ cup brown sugar
⅓ cup cooking oil
1 tablespoon milk
1 egg

1. Preheat oven to 375° F.
2. Wash blueberries from tin and drain on a paper towel. Set aside.
3. In a medium-size bowl, mix together blueberry muffin mix, oats, brown sugar, cooking oil, milk, and egg.
4. Drop by teaspoonfuls onto greased cookie sheets. Using a finger, press down in the center of each cookie and fill hole with 7 or 8 blueberries. Push batter from sides to cover up blueberries and then pat down.
5. Bake for 9 to 11 minutes, until light brown.

Yield: approximately 2½ dozen cookies

A popular slang phrase in England during the sixteenth and seventeenth centuries was "all the world is oatmeal." This meant, not surprisingly, that everything is delightful.

How true . . . how true!

• OATMEAL COOKIES FROM MARS •

Cathy Swerdlow
Longwood, Florida

½ cup butter or margarine
¾ cup sugar
1 egg
1 egg white
½ teaspoon vanilla
1½ cups all-purpose flour
1 teaspoon cinnamon

½ teaspoon baking soda
1 cup uncooked rolled oats
1 cup coarsely shredded unpeeled zucchini
1 cup chopped walnuts or pecans
1 cup semi-sweet chocolate chips

1. Preheat oven to 350° F.
2. Using an electric mixer, beat butter until softened. Add sugar and beat until fluffy. Add in egg, egg white, and vanilla, beating well. Set aside.
3. Stir together flour, cinnamon, and baking soda. Set mixer on low speed and gradually add flour mixture to cream mixture. Using a wooden spoon, stir in oats, zucchini, nuts, and chocolate chips.
4. Drop by rounded teaspoonfuls about 2 inches apart onto greased cookie sheets.
5. Bake for 10 to 12 minutes, until golden brown. Be careful not to over-bake.

Yield: approximately 4 dozen cookies

One of the most important and newsworthy aspects of the 1992 presidential election campaign was the crucial debate over who made the better chocolate chip cookies, Barbara Bush or Hillary Rodham Clinton.

Regardless of which candidate or political party you preferred, it should be noted that both Mrs. Bush's and Mrs. Clinton's cookies contained oatmeal and, therefore, were more correctly oatmeal–chocolate chip cookies rather than just plain chocolate chip cookies.

The importance of the inclusion of oatmeal in both cookies is validated by an article on the cookie conflict in *Newsweek* magazine, which pointed out there was a "secret" ingredient in both cookies: the oatmeal.

And you thought that choosing the president of the United States was based on assessing the national economy, foreign policy, legislative programs, and who had the better haircut.

◆ MOCHA MERINGUE KISSES ◆

Karen Nicholes McVarish
Davis, California

1 cup uncooked rolled oats
¾ cup almonds
¼ cup cocoa powder
1 teaspoon instant coffee powder
3 egg whites

dash salt
2¼ cups confectioners' sugar
1 tablespoon brandy
cocoa powder

1. In a large skillet, toast oats over medium-high heat for about 5 minutes, stirring continuously, until they begin to brown. Remove from heat and process in a food processor until toasted oats have the texture of whole wheat flour. Set aside.

2. In the same skillet, toast almonds over medium-high heat for about 3 minutes and then remove from heat and add to oats in food processor. Process mixture until almonds are finely ground. Remove from processor and stir in cocoa powder and coffee powder. Set aside.

3. Whip together egg whites and salt until they hold a soft peak. Slowly beat in confectioners' sugar and brandy and continue beating until stiff peaks form. Gently fold in oat mixture by hand.

4. Drop by teaspoonfuls 1 inch apart onto cookie sheets lined with parchment paper. Secure parchment paper with a small dab of batter at each corner.

5. Sprinkle each cookie with a light dusting of cocoa powder and then set aside to dry for 2 or 3 hours, until cookies are no longer sticky to the touch.

6. Preheat oven to 300° F. Bake for 25 minutes.

Yield: approximately 3 dozen cookies

According to Jane Hurley, a nutritionist with the Center for the Public Interest in Washington, D.C., and quoted in the February 17, 1993, issue of the *New York Times*, "Whether rolled or steel cut, even instant, oatmeal is a pretty perfect food. It's low fat, low cholesterol and salt free."

• HEART-SMART OATMEAL COOKIES •

Louise King
Grass Valley, California

6 figs
¼ cup extra virgin olive oil
¼ cup dark molasses
¼ cup honey
1 cup applesauce
1 teaspoon cinnamon
½ teaspoon ground ginger
½ teaspoon pumpkin pie spice
2 cups whole wheat flour

2 teaspoons baking powder
½ teaspoon salt
2½ cups uncooked rolled oats
4 large dates, chopped
cinnamon redhots, crushed peppermint
    candy, or glacé fruits used in
    fruitcakes

1. Soak figs in water overnight, then drain and purée in a blender.
2. Preheat oven to 375° F.
3. Using an electric mixer, combine figs, olive oil, molasses, honey, applesauce, cinnamon, ginger, and pumpkin pie spice. Add in flour, baking powder, and salt, mixing well. Add oats and dates, mixing in by hand.
4. Drop by teaspoonfuls onto cookie sheets lightly coated with olive oil spray.

5. Garnish each cookie with cinnamon redhots, crushed peppermint candy, or glacé fruits.

6. Bake for 15 to 20 minutes.

Yield: approximately 6 dozen cookies

Think of Quaker Oats and the actor Wilford Brimley comes instantly to mind, admonishing you to eat your oatmeal because "It's the right thing to do."

And it must be the right thing to do, because there has been a significant transformation in Mr. Brimley's activities in the commercials. For the last several years he has extolled the virtues of oatmeal while doing some pretty tame stuff like sitting at the kitchen table or walking the dog.

In the newest ads, there is a remarkable change showing what eating oatmeal will do for you. Mr. Brimley is seen in Western settings riding horses, digging postholes for a new corral, and engaging in similar strenuous endeavors.

But this change is not completely out of character for the actor. Mr. Brimley started in movies as a stuntman and is now, indeed, a rancher in real life when he is not appearing in films.

According to James Jordan, chairman of Jordan, McGrath, Case & Taylor, the advertising agency that created the Quaker Oats advertisements, Wilford Brimley is "a legitimate honest-to-God cowboy. [He] has more gold buckles, the principal award at rodeos, than Imelda Marcos has pairs of shoes."

• BEST-EVER CHIP CHIPS •

Nancy Sorenson
Smyrna, Georgia

1 cup margarine
1 cup cooking oil
1 cup firmly packed brown sugar
1 cup sugar
3 cups flour
1 egg
2 teaspoons vanilla

1 teaspoon salt
1 teaspoon cream of tartar
1½ cups uncooked rolled oats
1 cup flaked coconut
2 cups crisp rice cereal
1 cup chocolate chips
1 cup butterscotch chips

1. Preheat oven to 350° F.
2. Mix together margarine, oil, brown sugar, and sugar, beating until creamy. Beat in flour, egg, vanilla, salt, and cream of tartar. Stir in oats, coconut, cereal, chocolate chips, and butterscotch chips.
3. Drop by teaspoonfuls onto greased cookie sheets.
4. Bake for 10 to 12 minutes.

Yield: approximately 12 dozen cookies

• PEANUT BUTTER OATMEAL CRUNCH COOKIES •

Jennell Sylte
Sisseton, South Dakota

1 cup butter-flavored shortening
2 cups firmly packed brown sugar
1 cup extra-chunky peanut butter
4 egg whites, slightly beaten
1 teaspoon vanilla
2 cups all-purpose flour

1 teaspoon baking soda
½ teaspoon baking powder
2 cups crisp rice cereal
1½ cups chopped peanuts
1 cup uncooked quick rolled oats
1 cup flaked coconut

1. Preheat oven to 350° F.

2. Using an electric mixer set at medium speed, cream together shortening, brown sugar, and peanut butter in a large bowl. Beat in egg whites and vanilla. Set aside.

3. Stir together flour, baking soda, and baking powder. Add to cream mixture at low speed, until just blended.

4. Using a spoon, stir in one at a time rice cereal, peanuts, oats, and coconut.

5. Drop by rounded tablespoonfuls 2 inches apart onto greased cookie sheets.

6. Bake for 8 to 10 minutes, until set. Remove cookies immediately from cookie sheets and let cool on wire rack.

Yield: approximately 6 dozen cookies

Two of the more attractive places to eat oatmeal would be Oatlands, a city in Tasmania, the island state off the southeast coast of Australia, and Oatlands, a small town in Cape Province, South Africa.

You might also consider the city of Haverhill, Massachusetts, located thirty miles directly north of Boston, right on the New Hampshire border. That city could also be called Oathill, Massachusetts, since the people in northern England used to use the word "haver" for oats.

In the same way, "haversacks" got their name because of the cloth bags used to feed oats to horses.

• OATMEAL CHOCOLATE CHIPPERS •

Mary K. Mitchell
Battle Creek, Michigan

1 cup margarine, softened
¾ cup firmly packed brown sugar
¾ cup sugar
2 large eggs
1 teaspoon hot water
1 teaspoon vanilla
1½ cups all-purpose flour

1 teaspoon baking soda
1 teaspoon salt
2 cups uncooked quick rolled oats
1 cup flaked coconut
1 cup chopped pecans
1½ cups chocolate chips

1. Preheat oven to 375° F.
2. In a large bowl, cream together margarine, brown sugar, and sugar. Add eggs, one at a time, mixing well. Add water and vanilla, blending well. Mix in flour, baking soda, salt, oats, coconut, nuts, and chocolate chips.
3. Drop by rounded teaspoonfuls onto greased cookie sheets.
4. Bake for 10 to 12 minutes, until lightly browned around the edges and soft in the center. Remove immediately from cookie sheets to wax paper to cool.

Yield: approximately 6 dozen cookies

The phrase "feeling one's oats," meaning feeling really good and lively, comes from having a horse that is "full of oats" who feels satisfied and healthy.

Considering the important place that horses have had in America, it is just a small jump to go from a horse "feeling his oats" to a person "feeling his or her oats."

• CRANBERRY CHUNK COOKIES •

Helen Wolt
Colorado Springs, Colorado

1½ cups all-purpose flour
1 cup rolled or quick rolled oats
½ teaspoon baking soda
¼ teaspoon salt
1 teaspoon orange peel
½ cup butter
½ cup sugar
½ cup brown sugar

1 large egg
1 teaspoon vanilla
¼ cup milk
1 cup dried or fresh cranberries, chopped
1 cup white chocolate chunks or vanilla chips
¼ cup pecans or walnuts, chopped

1. Preheat oven to 350° F.
2. Stir together flour, oats, baking soda, salt, and orange peel. Set aside.
3. Using an electric mixer, cream together butter, sugar, and brown sugar until smooth. Add egg, blending until light and fluffy. Stir in vanilla and milk. Add flour mixture, stirring until just combined. Add cranberries, white chocolate chunks, and nuts.
4. Drop by large rounded tablespoonfuls 1½ inches apart onto greased cookie sheets.

5. Bake for 12 to 14 minutes, until golden around edges.

Yield: approximately 3 dozen large cookies

Thanks to Henry Ford, who began producing the Model T in 1908, the automobile became more and more common throughout the United States. Starting around 1910, the phrase "Oats for the donkey" became popular and referred to the money that was spent on operating and maintaining your new car.

· CARAMEL OATMEAL BARS ·

Tena Hawkins Huckleby
Greenville, Tennessee

1 cup butter or margarine
½ cup firmly packed brown sugar
½ cup sugar
2 egg yolks
½ cup chopped raisins

1 cup all-purpose flour, sifted
1 cup uncooked rolled oats
Caramel Topping (recipe follows)
½ cup chopped nuts

1. Preheat oven to 350° F.
2. Mix together butter, brown sugar, sugar, and egg yolks. Stir in raisins. Mix in flour and oats.
3. Using slightly dampened hands, spread batter onto the bottom of a greased and floured 9-inch by 13-inch pan.
4. Bake for 20 to 25 minutes. Remove from oven and let cool for 10 minutes. Spread Caramel Topping over top and then sprinkle with nuts. Cut into 1-inch by 2-inch bars.

Yield: approximately 4 dozen bars

CARAMEL TOPPING

14 ounces caramel candies　　　　　*2 tablespoons butter*

Melt caramels and butter over hot water and stir together well.

Despite the growing popularity of oatmeal and oat bran as healthy foods in the last few years, during the last twenty-five years the amount of oats grown in the United States has decreased by nearly 75 percent.

The reason for this apparent contradiction is that only a very small percentage—about 5 percent—of all the oats grown are used for human consumption. Most of the other 95 percent of the oats produced has been used as feed for livestock, but recently feeds better than just oats for livestock have been developed so fewer oats need to be grown.

• APRICOT-FILLED OATMEAL COOKIES •

Carolyn E. Popwell
Lacey, Washington

1½ cups sugar
½ cup molasses
¾ cup butter or margarine, melted
2 large eggs
2 cups all-purpose flour
3 cups uncooked rolled oats or
  quick rolled oats

1 teaspoon baking soda
½ teaspoon salt
⅓ cup chopped almonds, toasted
Apricot Filling (recipe follows)

1. Preheat oven to 375° F.
2. Mix together sugar, molasses, butter, and eggs. Stir in flour, oats, baking soda, salt, and toasted almonds.
3. Set aside one-third of the batter. Drop the remaining portion of the batter by rounded teaspoonfuls 2½ inches apart onto lightly greased cookie sheets. Flatten cookies with the bottom of a dampened glass dipped in sugar.
4. Top each cookie with ½ teaspoon Apricot Filling and then cover with a teaspoon of batter taken from the remaining one-third portion.
5. Bake for 10 to 12 minutes, until golden.

Yield: approximately 4 dozen cookies

APRICOT FILLING

2 cups dried apricots, chopped　　*½ cup water*
¾ cup sugar　　*⅓ cup chopped almonds, toasted*

1. Heat apricots, sugar, and water in a heavy saucepan over medium heat to boiling. Stir occasionally and cook until mixture thickens, about 6 minutes.
2. Remove from heat, stir in almonds, and then let cool.

"Truly, a peck of provender: I could munch your good dry oats."
—William Shakespeare, from *A Midsummer Night's Dream*

• ROSY ROCKS •

Frances Concetta Kauffman
Edgewater Park, New Jersey

1½ cups all-purpose flour
1 teaspoon baking powder
½ teaspoon baking soda
2 teaspoons cinnamon
1 teaspoon allspice
1⅓ cups sugar
1 cup shortening

1 egg
1 10¾-ounce can condensed tomato
    soup
2 cups uncooked rolled oats
1 cup raisins
1 cup chopped walnuts

1. Preheat oven to 350° F.
2. Sift together flour, baking powder, baking soda, cinnamon, and allspice. Mix in sugar. Add shortening, egg, and soup, beating with an electric mixer set at medium speed for 2 minutes. Scrape sides and bottom of bowl often. Stir in oats, raisins, and nuts.
3. Drop by rounded teaspoonfuls onto greased cookie sheets.
4. Bake for 14 to 16 minutes, until light brown.

Yield: approximately 7 dozen cookies

George Bush's aversion to broccoli has been well publicized, but one of the things the former president did eat got less publicity. And it was considerably different from any green vegetable most people have ever seen.

The rather unusual meal enjoyed by President Bush was a breakfast of a bowl of oatmeal with a Butterfinger candy bar crumbled on top.

• BROWNIE OAT COOKIES •

Megan M. Barsel
Delran, New Jersey

1 cup uncooked quick rolled oats	1 teaspoon baking powder
⅔ cup flour	2 egg whites
⅔ cup sugar	⅓ cup light or dark corn syrup
⅓ cup cocoa powder	1 teaspoon vanilla

1. Preheat oven to 350° F.
2. In a large bowl, combine oats, flour, sugar, cocoa powder, and baking powder. Mix together well. Add egg whites, corn syrup, and vanilla. Mix well. (Batter will be thick.)
3. Drop by teaspoonfuls onto cookie sheets lightly coated with cooking spray.
4. Bake for 9 to 11 minutes.

Yield: approximately 3½ dozen cookies

Please note that if you are reading some very early literary works, say those written before the thirteenth century, "oat" was written as "ote" with the plural being "otes" or "oten."

And the combination "oatmeal" came from Middle English around 1400, joining together "ote" and "mele."

• DOROTHY'S BRANDIED OATIES •

Dorothy M. Rogers
Bellevue, Nebraska

1½ cups golden raisins
1 cup water
½ cup margarine
1 cup sugar
½ cup brandy
2 eggs, beaten
1 teaspoon baking soda

2 cups uncooked rolled oats
2½ cups unbleached white flour
½ teaspoon baking powder
½ teaspoon ground nutmeg
½ teaspoon salt
2 cups chopped walnuts

1. Preheat oven to 350° F.
2. Combine raisins and water in a large microwave bowl. Microwave on high for 5 minutes. Remove bowl from microwave oven and add margarine. Stir until melted. Add in sugar, brandy, eggs, baking soda, oats, flour, baking powder, nutmeg, salt, and walnuts. Mix together well.
3. Drop by teaspoonfuls onto greased cookie sheets.
4. Bake for 9 to 11 minutes. Watch carefully since cookies can burn easily.

Yield: approximately 5 dozen cookies

Charles Kingsley, an English author and clergyman who lived from 1819 to 1875, noted shortly before his death that oatmeal is invaluable for growing children.

• ENGLISH MATRIMONIALS •

Millie Shirley
Port Orange, Florida

1½ cups flour
1¼ cups uncooked rolled oats
1 cup brown sugar

¾ cup butter, softened
¾ cup seedless raspberry or strawberry
jam

1. Preheat oven to 325° F.
2. Mix together flour, oats, and brown sugar. Blend in butter until mixture is crumbly.
3. Press one-half of batter onto the bottom of a lightly greased 8-inch square or 9-inch square pan. Spread jam evenly over batter. Lightly press remaining batter over top of jam.
4. Bake for 35 to 40 minutes, until golden brown. Remove from oven, let cool, and then cut into 1½-inch squares.

Yield: approximately 2½ dozen squares

"The vices of youth are varnished over by the saying that there must be time for 'sowing of wild oats.' "
—William Cobbett (English journalist and social reformer, born 1763—died 1835, in his *Advice to Young Men*, written in 1829)

Actually, the phrase "To sow wild oats," meaning to commit youthful excesses or follies and to spend one's early life in dissipation, can be traced back to mid-sixteenth-century England. Its origin was in the foolishness and mischief of sowing wild oats instead of good grain.

Further slander of the good name of oats came in the eighteenth century in England when "oatmeal" became the slang term for boisterous young men because the author of a ludicrous and bizarre pamphlet of that time used the pen name Oliver Oat-meale.

· CHA'S "GOT A DATE WITH A SPICY MAC-OATMEAL COOKIE" ·

Cha Grenn
Las Vegas, Nevada

¼ cup butter, softened
¼ cup all-vegetable shortening
¼ cup peanut butter
¼ cup honey
½ cup light brown sugar
½ cup sugar
1 large egg, lightly beaten
1 teaspoon vanilla
1 cup all-purpose flour
½ teaspoon reduced-sodium salt
½ teaspoon baking soda

1 tablespoon cocoa powder
½ teaspoon cinnamon
½ teaspoon ground ginger
¼ teaspoon ground cloves
¼ teaspoon ground nutmeg
¾ cup flaked coconut
1 cup uncooked quick rolled oats
1 cup chopped dates
1 cup coarsely chopped macadamia
nuts

1. Preheat oven to 350° F.
2. In a large bowl, cream together butter, shortening, peanut butter, honey, brown sugar, and sugar until light. Beat in egg and vanilla. Set aside.
3. Sift together flour, salt, baking soda, cocoa powder, cinnamon, ginger, cloves, and nutmeg. Gradually add to cream mixture, combining thoroughly. Fold in coconut, oats, dates, and nuts.

4. Using a cookie scoop or a teaspoon, drop cookie batter 1 inch apart onto cookie sheets that have been lightly coated with vegetable oil cooking spray.

5. Bake for 13 to 14 minutes, until slightly browned on bottom. Remove cookies from cookie sheets and let cool on wire rack.

Yield: approximately 3½ dozen cookies

Next time you are having oatmeal for breakfast, think about this: About 42 million bushels of oats are used each year in the United States to make breakfast foods.

• COCONUT CRISPIES •

Donna Dyke
Port Colborne, Ontario, Canada

1⅓ cups all-purpose flour
1 teaspoon baking powder
½ teaspoon baking soda
½ teaspoon salt
1 cup brown sugar
½ cup butter or margarine

½ cup vegetable shortening
1 egg
1 teaspoon vanilla
1½ cups uncooked rolled oats
¾ cup flaked coconut

1. Preheat oven to 375° F.
2. Stir together flour, baking powder, baking soda, and salt. Set aside.
3. Cream together brown sugar, butter, shortening, egg, and vanilla, mixing thoroughly. Add flour mixture to cream mixture. Stir in oats and coconut.
4. Drop by teaspoonfuls 2 inches apart onto lightly greased cookie sheets. Flatten each cookie with a fork that has been dipped in flour.
5. Bake for 10 to 15 minutes, until golden.

Yield: approximately 5 dozen cookies

Under the heading of "What won't they think of next?" the Taiwan Sugu Company in Taipei, Taiwan, has invented the first edible tableware.

The bowls and plates are made of oatmeal and can be eaten after they are used. And just like real china, the oatmeal dishes have a glossy finish. The company is also planning to market edible spoons and boxes to replace the Styrofoam boxes used by fast-food chains. One drawback to the oatmeal tableware is that the bowls start to leak three or four hours after coming into contact with boiling water.

Hey, nothing's perfect.

• THE COMMODORE'S OATMEAL COOKIES •

Florence P. Didion
Toledo, Ohio

2 cups unsifted flour
1 teaspoon baking powder
1 cup vegetable shortening
1 cup sugar
1 cup light brown sugar
2 eggs, slightly beaten

1 teaspoon baking soda, dissolved in 3
  tablespoons wine or whiskey
2 cups wheat or corn flake cereal
2 cups uncooked rolled oats
1 cup coarsely chopped nuts
1 cup raisins

1. Preheat oven to 350° F.
2. Sift together flour and baking powder. Mix in shortening, sugar, brown sugar, eggs, baking soda dissolved in wine or whiskey, cereal, oats, chopped nuts, and raisins.
3. Drop by tablespoonfuls onto lightly greased cookie sheets.
4. Bake for 13 to 15 minutes, until light brown.

Yield: approximately 6½ dozen cookies

Oatmeal is available in the store in three different versions: old-fashioned oats, quick-cooking oats, and instant oats.

Old-fashioned oats are whole oats that are steamed and flattened into rolled oats but remain uncut. Quick-cooking oats are cut in order to shorten the time needed to cook them. And instant oats have been cut into even smaller pieces and processed so they can be prepared just by adding boiling water.

• ALLIE-OOPS •

Peggy Oye
Allison Oye
Tuscola, Illinois

1 cup butter or margarine, softened
1 cup peanut butter
1 cup applesauce
1 cup sugar
½ cup brown sugar
2 eggs, beaten

1 teaspoon vanilla
2 cups uncooked rolled oats
2 teaspoons baking soda
3 cups flour
3 cups m&m's chocolate candies

1. Preheat oven to 325° F.
2. In a large mixing bowl, combine butter, peanut butter, applesauce, sugar, and brown sugar. Beat until creamy. Add eggs and vanilla. Stir in oats.
3. Combine baking soda and flour and add to cream mixture. Stir in m&m's chocolate candies.
4. Drop by tablespoonfuls onto a greased cookie sheet.
5. Bake for 12 to 15 minutes, until golden brown.

Yield: approximately 6 dozen cookies

An important part of the advertising for any product is its packaging and the words printed there to entice you to buy it. So it should be no surprise that on the front of each box of Cheerios (made by General Mills) is the line "Made from Whole Grain Oats." And on the side panel of the box is the additional tag line "Made from the Grain Highest in Protein."

Going a step further, Kellogg's Cracklin' Oat Bran cereal box displays the highest praise possible and the most persuasive reason of all to make the best purchase:

Great!
Oatmeal
Cookie Taste

General Mills and Kellogg's know that consumers will do the right thing.

• FRUIT AND NUT GOODNESS COOKIES •

Sharon Harris
Saint Louis, Missouri

2 cups flour
1 teaspoon baking powder
1 teaspoon baking soda
dash salt
½ cup brown sugar
½ cup sugar
1 cup margarine
2 eggs

1 8¼-ounce can crushed pineapple
   with juice, undrained
1 tablespoon banana liqueur
2 cups uncooked rolled oats
¾ cup flaked coconut
¾ cup chopped dates
1 cup chopped macadamia nuts

1. Preheat oven to 375° F.
2. Stir together flour, baking powder, baking soda, and salt. Set aside.
3. Beat together brown sugar, sugar, margarine, and eggs. Stir in pineapple with juice and banana liqueur. Blend in flour mixture. Add oats, coconut, dates, and macadamia nuts, mixing together well.
4. Drop by teaspoonfuls onto greased cookie sheets.
5. Bake for 12 to 15 minutes. Remove from oven and let cool on wire racks.

Yield: approximately 6 dozen cookies

Back in the late 1980s when news began to spread about the cholesterol-reducing ability of oats, there was an explosion in demand for any kind of food that contained oats.

At this time, The Real Food Company in San Francisco tripled their sales of bulk oat bran, while at Alfalfa's Market in Boulder, Colorado, sales of oatmeal cookies and breakfast cereals made with oats increased by 500 percent.

• BREAKFAST YUM-YUMS •

Anne T. Waldrop
Decatur, Georgia

⅔ cup margarine, softened
⅔ cup sugar
1 egg
1 teaspoon vanilla
¾ cup flour
½ teaspoon baking soda

½ teaspoon salt
1½ cups uncooked rolled oats
1 cup shredded cheddar cheese
½ cup wheat germ
6 slices cooked bacon, crumbled, or
　　bacon-flavored chips

1. Preheat oven to 350° F.
2. Mix together margarine, sugar, egg, and vanilla. Add in flour, baking soda, and salt. Stir in oats, cheese, wheat germ, and bacon. Batter will be stiff.
3. Drop by tablespoonfuls onto greased cookie sheets.
4. Bake for 12 to 14 minutes. Remove from oven and let cool for 1 minute before removing from cookie sheets.

Yield: approximately 3 dozen cookies

In his column "On Language" in the *New York Times Magazine*, William Safire notes the mixed metaphor put forward by James R. Sasser, the Democratic senator from Tennessee. Senator Sasser was praising President Bill Clinton's knowledge of domestic issues and lauded his party's leader by saying "This guy knows his oats."

Louis Jay Herman, one of Mr. Safire's more observant readers—a member of the Gotcha! Gangsters, as Mr. Safire calls those who point out fractures of the English language—noted that "Mr. Clinton may be feeling his oats, but he knows his onions."

• OAT DROPS •

Susie Tibbetts
Hamburg, New York

¼ cup margarine
1 cup milk
½ teaspoon salt
4 cups sugar
4 ounces unsweetened chocolate

2 teaspoons vanilla
1 cup peanut butter
4 cups uncooked rolled oats
½ cup nuts

1. In a heavy saucepan, combine margarine, milk, salt, sugar, and chocolate. Heat to boiling and let boil for 1 minute while stirring constantly.
2. Remove from heat and add vanilla, peanut butter, oats, and nuts. Let cool slightly.
3. Drop by teaspoonfuls onto wax paper.
4. Chill in refrigerator until firm.

Yield: approximately 4 dozen cookies

Convenience foods are thought of as modern inventions with their origin in the TV dinners of the 1950s. The truth is that thirty years earlier, Quick Cooking Quaker Oats were introduced as a convenience food to save time and make preparing breakfast easier than before.

• CHOCO-NUT CHEWS •

Mrs. Clarence Brost
Wheeling, West Virginia

1½ cups uncooked quick rolled oats
14 ounces sweetened condensed
   milk
1 teaspoon vanilla
½ teaspoon salt
½ teaspoon cinnamon

½ teaspoon ground nutmeg
2¾ cups semi-sweet chocolate chips
½ cup chunky peanut butter
Fudge Frosting (recipe follows)
⅓ cup chopped peanuts

1. Preheat oven to 350° F.
2. Beat together oats, condensed milk, vanilla, salt, cinnamon, and nutmeg. Add chocolate chips and peanut butter, blending well. Batter will be stiff.
3. Spread batter in a greased 8-inch square pan.
4. Bake for 25 to 30 minutes. Remove from oven and let cool. Top with Fudge Frosting and sprinkle with chopped peanuts. Cut into 1¼-inch by 1¼-inch squares.

Yield: approximately 3 dozen bars

FUDGE FROSTING

3 ounces semi-sweet chocolate   *1 teaspoon vanilla*
1½ tablespoons milk

1. Melt chocolate with milk over hot, not boiling, water.
2. Remove from heat and stir in vanilla.

• OATKINS •

Kathy L. Eastman
Tempe, Arizona

¾ cup margarine, softened
1 cup brown sugar
1 cup sugar
4 egg whites
1¼ cups canned pumpkin
2¾ cups all-purpose flour
1 teaspoon baking powder
½ teaspoon salt

¼ teaspoon ground cloves
¼ teaspoon allspice
1½ teaspoons cinnamon
3 cups rolled oats or quick rolled oats
¾ cup chopped dates
¾ cup raisins

1. Preheat oven to 350° F.

2. Using an electric mixer, in a large bowl beat together margarine, brown sugar, and sugar until creamy. Beat in egg whites and pumpkin. Set aside.

3. Stir together flour, baking powder, salt, cloves, allspice, and cinnamon. Gradually add to butter mixture, blending thoroughly. Mix in oats, dates, and raisins.

4. Drop by rounded teaspoonfuls about 1 inch apart onto cookie sheets coated with nonstick cooking spray.

5. Bake for 13 to 15 minutes, until edges are light brown. Remove from cookie sheets and let cool on wire racks.

Yield: approximately 6½ dozen cookies

How popular is oatmeal . . . and not just in steaming bowls and in cookies?

Sappo Hill Soapworks on Tolman Creek Road in Ashland, Oregon, a small town in the southern part of the state just over the California border, offers an attractive variety of all-vegetable-oil glycerine creme soaps.

The soaps come in a spectacular assortment of colors and fragrances:

- white soap with almond fragrance
- green soap with aloe vera fragrance
- pink soap with cascade rose fragrance
- light green with cucumber fragrance
- violet with jasmine fragrance
- blue soap with Oregon berry fragrance
- dusty gold with sandalwood fragrance
- vanilla with spicy pear fragrance

Given this great selection of appealing and seductive soaps, it is gratifying to see that the best-selling soap from Sappo Hill Soapworks is their oatmeal soap, which has a grainy texture and contains rolled oats.

And best of all, whenever you use this popular soap you are rewarded with the aroma of nothing less than oatmeal cookies!

In the early days of commercial radio, many people listened to this new wonder of information and entertainment on radios that looked just like boxes of Quaker Oats cereal. The company offered an easy-to-use portable crystal radio set as a promotional item that you could get for one dollar and two Quaker Oats trademarks cut from any two packages of the company's products.

♦ CHRISTMAS COOKIES ♦

Lella Perrault
Saint Paul, Minnesota

1 cup butter
1½ cups sugar
2 eggs
2 cups flour
1 teaspoon baking soda
1 teaspoon salt
1 teaspoon cinnamon

2 cups uncooked quick rolled oats
2 tablespoons wine
1½ cups chopped dates
1½ cups candied cherries
1½ cups candied pineapple
4 cups chopped pecans

1. Preheat oven to 350° F.
2. Cream together butter and sugar. Add in eggs, mixing well. Add flour, baking soda, salt, cinnamon, and oats. Fold in wine, dates, cherries, pineapple, and pecans.
3. Drop by rounded teaspoonfuls onto greased cookie sheets.
4. Bake for 10 to 12 minutes. Do not overbake.

Yield: approximately 8 dozen cookies

Ferdinand Schumacher may not be a household name today, but he was well known as "The Oatmeal King" in America after starting the German Mills American Oatmeal Company in 1856. In 1901 this company merged with two others to become Quaker Oats.

• BUTTERSCOTCH BANANA DROPS •

Marg Holt
Fargo, North Dakota

¾ cup shortening
1 cup sugar
1 egg
1 cup mashed bananas
1¾ cups uncooked rolled oats
1½ cups flour

½ teaspoon baking soda
1 teaspoon salt
¼ teaspoon ground nutmeg
¾ teaspoon cinnamon
2 cups butterscotch chips

1. Preheat oven to 400° F.
2. Cream together shortening and sugar until light and fluffy. Add egg and beat well. Mix in bananas and oats. Add flour, baking soda, salt, nutmeg, and cinnamon. Blend in butterscotch chips.
3. Drop by teaspoonfuls onto greased cookie sheets.
4. Bake for 13 to 15 minutes. Remove cookies immediately from cookie sheets.

Yield: approximately 4 dozen cookies

Most people automatically associate oatmeal with Quaker Oats and its distinctive packaging.

In 1877, Quaker Oats was sold as the first trademarked breakfast cereal in the United States, and sold it in bulk in both the United States and Great Britain.

The company advertised heavily and even used poetry to extol the virtues of its cereal. In its poem titled "Joy" which appeared in newspaper advertisements during the 1890s, the concluding line ran: "When breakfast's called in cheery notes, I eat my dish of Quaker Oats."

One of the marketing techniques introduced by Quaker Oats was sending free trial-sized samples directly to consumers. In 1891, half-ounce boxes of Quaker Oats were delivered to every mailbox in Portland, Oregon. The response was immediate, and the demand was so great that Quaker Oats had to rush 252,000 pounds of the cereal by train from its plant in Iowa to Portland.

• OATMEAL TRILBYS •

Margaret Carlson
Amery, Wisconsin

1 cup brown sugar
½ cup butter
½ cup shortening
1½ teaspoons baking soda
½ cup sour cream
1 egg

1 teaspoon vanilla
2 cups uncooked rolled oats
2 cups flour
½ teaspoon salt
Date Filling (recipe follows)

1. Preheat oven to 350° F.
2. Cream together sugar, butter, and shortening. Set aside.
3. Mix baking soda into the sour cream. Stir in egg and vanilla. Add to cream mixture. Stir in oats, flour, and salt.
4. Drop by tablespoonfuls onto lightly greased cookie sheets. Flatten cookies with the bottom of a dampened glass.
5. Bake for 10 to 12 minutes, until slightly browned. Remove from oven and let cool.
6. Spread Date Filling on flat sides of cookies and make sandwiches. For crispy cookie sandwiches, do not put Date Filling on until just before serving.

Yield: approximately 2 dozen large sandwich cookies

DATE FILLING

½ cup sugar
1½ cups dates

½ cup water

1. Combine sugar, dates, and water in a heavy saucepan and cook over medium heat until sugar completely dissolves and mixture becomes thick.
2. Remove from heat and let cool.

A spy in 1614, observing the activities at the Jamestown colony in what would later become Virginia, reported that the residents were surviving on just one grain: oats.

· MALTED OATMEAL BARS ·

E. M. Weber
Collegeville, Pennsylvania

½ cup butter or margarine
1 cup sugar
2 eggs
1 teaspoon vanilla
½ cup sifted all-purpose flour

½ cup chocolate malted milk powder
¼ teaspoon salt
¾ cup uncooked quick rolled oats
½ cup chopped walnuts

1. Preheat oven to 350° F.
2. Cream together butter and sugar. Add eggs and vanilla, beating well. Set aside.
3. Sift together flour, malted milk powder, and salt. Combine thoroughly with cream mixture. Stir in oats and walnuts.
4. Using slightly dampened hands, spread batter into an 8-inch or a 9-inch square pan.
5. Bake for 33 to 37 minutes. Remove from oven, let cool, and cut into 1½-inch by 2-inch bars.

Yield: approximately 2 dozen bars

One of the folk legends of Eastern Europe is the Oats Goat, which is the field spirit of growing oats. Parents warned their children to stay out of the oat fields or the Oats Goat would get them. And in some places the people reaping the oats are said to do their work extra fast to get themselves ahead of the Oats Goat, who pushes along any worker not reaping fast enough.

◆ OATMEAL SNACK BARS ◆

Mrs. Dorothy Duty
Pasadena, Texas

1½ cups uncooked rolled oats
¾ cup flour
¼ cup sugar
½ cup firmly packed brown sugar

¾ cup margarine
1 pound cream cheese
2 eggs
Apple Topping (recipe follows)

1. Preheat oven to 350° F.
2. Mix together oats, flour, sugar, and brown sugar. Cut in margarine, 1 tablespoon at a time, until coarsely mixed.
3. Spread all but 1 cup of mixture into a greased 9-inch by 13-inch pan.
4. Bake for 15 minutes. Remove from oven.
5. Mix together cream cheese and eggs and spread evenly over cooked crust.
6. Sprinkle Apple Topping evenly over cream cheese layer. Sprinkle remaining crust batter evenly over Apple Topping.
7. Return to oven and bake for 25 minutes more. Cut into 1½-inch by 2-inch bars and serve warm or cold.

Yield: approximately 3 dozen bars

APPLE TOPPING

1 cup chopped apples
⅓ cup raisins

1 tablespoon sugar
½ teaspoon cinnamon

Mix together well apples, raisins, sugar, and cinnamon.

The place: Bloomingdale's in Manhattan.

The time: shortly before Christmas, 1992.

The characters: a little girl making her annual holiday visit to the North Pole and a jolly bearded gentleman in a bright red suit.

The topic of conversation: favorite Christmas cookies.

The favorite cookies of the jolly bearded gentleman: chocolate chip and oatmeal.

◆ DOUBLE-DECKER DELIGHTS ◆

Alberta Sullivan
Columbus, Kansas

LOWER DECK

½ cup margarine, softened
½ cup shortening
1 cup brown sugar
1 cup sugar
½ cup cocoa powder
2 eggs

1½ teaspoons vanilla
1½ cups sifted flour
½ teaspoon salt
1¼ teaspoons baking soda
2 cups uncooked quick rolled oats

UPPER DECK

14 ounces sweetened condensed
  milk
1 teaspoon vanilla
¼ teaspoon almond extract
½ cup confectioners' sugar
1 cup sifted flour

dash salt
3½ cups flaked coconut
½ cup finely chopped pecans
2 egg whites, stiffly beaten
approximately 30 drained maraschino
  cherry halves

1. *To make Lower Deck:* Beat together margarine, shortening, brown sugar, and sugar until light and creamy. Stir in cocoa powder, eggs, and vanilla.

Blend together well. Add flour, salt, and baking soda. Stir in oats, blending well.

2. Divide batter in half. Using wax paper, shape batter into two logs, about 3 inches in diameter and 8 to 10 inches long.

3. Wrap logs and chill in refrigerator for at least 2 hours.

4. *To make Upper Deck:* Blend together condensed milk, vanilla, almond extract, confectioners' sugar, flour, salt, coconut, and pecans. Gently fold in egg whites.

5. Preheat oven to 325° F.

6. Remove Lower Deck logs from refrigerator. Slice into ½-inch rounds and place on greased cookie sheets about 2 inches apart. Press down lightly on each cookie.

7. Place 1 heaping teaspoon of Upper Deck mixture in center of each cookie. Lightly press maraschino cherry half onto top of cookie.

8. Bake for 18 to 22 minutes, until coconut is very lightly browned. Let cookies cool slightly before removing from cookie sheets. Place cookies on wax paper and let cool completely. Store in an airtight container.

Yield: approximately 2½ dozen cookies

The op-ed page of the august *New York Times* is usually reserved for serious discussions about foreign events, political philosophies, current affairs, economic policies, government activities, and similar weighty matters.

But on June 23, 1990, there was a poem by the author Galway Kinnell among the really serious stuff. The title of Mr. Kinnell's poem was "Oatmeal," and the first line read "I eat oatmeal for breakfast."

· BEBE'S NO-BAKES ·

Bernice K. Robertson
West Columbia, South Carolina

2 cups sugar	2½ cups uncooked rolled oats
¼ cup cocoa powder	½ cup peanut butter
½ cup milk	½ cup chopped dates
½ cup butter	2 teaspoons vanilla

1. In a heavy saucepan, mix together sugar, cocoa powder, milk, and butter. Heat to boiling and let boil for 1½ minutes.

2. Remove from heat and add oats, peanut butter, dates, and vanilla.

3. Drop by teaspoonfuls onto wax paper and let cool.

Yield: approximately 4 dozen cookies

In the May/June 1990 issue of *The Saturday Evening Post* is an essay written by Dr. Gustave H. Hoehn of San Gabriel, California. Dr. Hoehn writes about the nutritional value of oats and includes the following advice:

In fact, I tell a patient, if she will bake forty little bite-sized oatmeal cookies on her day off, she can slip one in her mouth conveniently and delicately while waiting for her ride or driving. They are not messy to carry or to handle, and if tiny, they can be very ladylike.

And what has she had? Good oatmeal with raisins and pecan or sunflower seeds—even some flax or poppy seed and a bit of nonhydrogenated oil and a bit of sugar and milk. That is almost identical to cereal in a bowl and cooked.

The concluding line by Dr. Hoehn, after giving many, many beneficial reasons for eating oats, is "Feed your children oats if you want them to be leaders; feed them corn and millet if you want them to be led."

• OREGON TRAIL BITS •

John C. Burk
Bliss, Idaho

2 cups margarine
2 cups brown sugar
2 cups sugar
2 teaspoons vanilla
4 large eggs
3½ cups flour
1 cup whole wheat flour

2 teaspoons baking powder
2 teaspoons baking soda
2 cups uncooked rolled oats
3 cups raisin bran cereal
1 to 2 cups chocolate chips
1 to 2 cups m&m's chocolate candies

1. Preheat oven to 350° F.
2. Cream together margarine, brown sugar, sugar, vanilla, and eggs. Set aside.
3. Stir together flour, wheat flour, baking powder, and baking soda. Combine with margarine mixture. Add in oats, raisin bran cereal, chocolate chips, and m&m's chocolate candies. Mix well.
4. Using a ¼-cup measuring cup, scoop out batter and place 4 or 5 cookies on each greased cookie sheet.
5. Bake for 14 to 16 minutes.

Yield: approximately 5 dozen large cookies

Oats are an important ingredient in many Scottish dishes, including porridge (the Scottish word for cooked breakfast cereal), scones, pancakes, and gingerbread. They are also used as a crispy coating for fried foods, as thickeners in soups, and in other traditional recipes including haggis, a sausage made from the innards of a sheep or a calf.

Although oats (called "oatmeal" in its uncooked form) have been and still are very popular in Scotland, they are not native to the land there. The Romans brought oats with them when they came to the British Isles. Oats prospered as one of the few crops that could survive and thrive in the cool and damp climate of Scotland.

• ALMOST INSTANT OATMEAL COOKIES •

Dr. Joseph A. Toth
South Bend, Indiana

½ cup butter
½ cup evaporated milk
2 cups sugar
1 teaspoon almond extract

2 cups uncooked quick rolled oats
1 cup ground pecans
1 cup chopped dates
confectioners' sugar

1. Place butter, milk, and sugar in a large saucepan and slowly heat to boiling. Add almond extract and oats, continuing to boil until oats are cooked.

2. Remove from heat and mix in pecans and dates. Let cool.

3. Drop by heaping tablespoonfuls onto wax paper, pressing each cookie with a spoon to flatten. Sprinkle generously with confectioners' sugar.

Yield: approximately 5 dozen cookies

• J'S OATMEAL COOKIES •

Mrs. S. L. Davis
Red Oak, Iowa

1 cup raisins
¾ cup water
1 cup vegetable shortening,
  margarine, or butter (or any
  combination)
1 cup sugar
3 eggs
2 cups flour

½ teaspoon salt
¾ teaspoon baking soda
¼ teaspoon ground cloves
½ teaspoon allspice
1 teaspoon cinnamon
2 cups uncooked quick rolled oats
1 cup nuts
½ cup chopped dates

1. Preheat oven to 350° F.
2. Place raisins and water in a heavy saucepan and bring to a boil. Cook only until raisins are plump, about 2 minutes.
3. Remove from heat and drain raisins, saving 6 tablespoons of the liquid. Set aside.
4. Using an electric mixer, cream together vegetable shortening and sugar for several minutes. Add eggs and continue mixing. Set aside.
5. Stir together flour, salt, baking soda, ground cloves, allspice, and cinnamon.
6. Add flour mixture to cream mixture, alternating with the 6 tablespoons

of liquid saved from cooking the raisins. Add cooked raisins, oats, nuts, and dates, mixing together well. If desired, batter can be chilled in refrigerator for about 1 hour for easier handling.

7. Drop by teaspoonfuls onto greased cookie sheets.
8. Bake for 8 to 10 minutes, until light brown.

Yield: approximately 5½ dozen cookies

There is no shortage of responsible sex and safe-sex messages around these days, including the following from California:

"Sow your wild oats . . . and pray for crop failure."

That slogan can be considered sort of a modern update of a line from Act IV of *Trinummus*, a play by the Roman comic poet Plautus who lived around 200 B.C.:

"A proper place for men to sow their wild oats—where they will not spring up."

• OATMEAL COOKIES CARIBBEAN •

Cheryl Galloway
Houston, Texas

1 cup margarine, softened
½ cup sugar
¾ cup firmly packed brown sugar
1 egg
⅓ cup rum
2 teaspoons vanilla
1½ cups whole wheat flour

1 teaspoon baking soda
¼ teaspoon salt
2 teaspoons cinnamon
1 teaspoon ground nutmeg
3 cups uncooked rolled oats
¾ cup pecans, chopped
¾ cup almonds, chopped

1. Preheat oven to 375° F.
2. Cream together margarine, sugar, and brown sugar. Beat in egg, rum, and vanilla. Mix in flour, baking soda, salt, cinnamon, and nutmeg. Stir in oats, pecans, and almonds.
3. Drop by heaping tablespoonfuls onto greased cookie sheets.
4. Bake for 8 to 10 minutes.

Yield: approximately 4 dozen cookies

When someone in eighteenth-century England said that he was going "to oat," he meant that he was going "to eat" as in, "I stopped by the diner and oated dinner . . . and then I oated an oatmeal cookie."

◆ HONEY APPLE COOKIES ◆

Joann Hight
Anchorage, Alaska

½ cup margarine, softened
½ cup honey
1 egg
1 teaspoon vanilla
¾ cup unsifted stone ground (whole grain) flour

½ teaspoon baking soda
¾ teaspoon cinnamon
1 medium apple, finely chopped
1½ cups uncooked rolled oats

1. Preheat oven to 375° F.
2. Beat together margarine, honey, egg, and vanilla. Set aside.
3. Mix together flour, baking soda, and cinnamon and add to margarine mixture. Add apple, mixing well. Stir in oats.
4. Drop by teaspoonfuls onto greased cookie sheets.
5. Bake for 10 minutes.

Yield: approximately 4 dozen cookies

Around the middle of the nineteenth century the phrase "to have not an oat" meant to be penniless, since an oat was considered to be something small.

· DELIGHT BITES ·

Elaine M. Piringer
Saint Paul, Minnesota

2 cups flour
1 teaspoon baking soda
1 teaspoon cinnamon
1 cup sugar
1 cup firmly packed brown sugar
1½ cups butter or margarine
¾ cup peanut butter
1 teaspoon vanilla

2 eggs, well beaten
2½ cups uncooked rolled oats
¼ cup milk
1 cup chocolate-covered raisin candies
½ cup chopped water chestnuts, well
   dried
½ cup chopped peanuts

1. Preheat oven to 350° F.

2. Sift together flour, baking soda, and cinnamon. Set aside.

3. In a large bowl, cream together sugar, brown sugar, butter, and peanut butter. Add vanilla and eggs, beating well. Gradually stir in flour mixture and oats, alternating with milk, beginning and ending with dry ingredients. Mix in raisin candies, water chestnuts, and peanuts.

4. Drop by heaping teaspoonfuls about 3 inches apart onto greased cookie sheets.

5. Bake for 10 to 12 minutes. Remove cookies from cookie sheets and let cool on wire rack.

Yield: approximately 7½ dozen cookies

Who eats oats?

Just about everyone, for as the old song says, "Mares eat oats and does eat oats."

Because horses play such an important part in Western movies, those movies became known in Hollywood as "oat operas" and "oaters."

And that is not the only semantic connection between horses and oats. Consider the following letter to the editor, published in the New York *Daily News* on August 20, 1952, which complains about taxes (yes, there were even complaints about taxes back then):

> "When the time comes . . . that even an oat-burner must sport a tax stamp on its stem or stern . . ."

There is even more in the connection between horses and oats.

Cowboy movie star Roy Rogers, long before he started selling fast-food hamburgers, roast beef, and French fries, was a celebrity spokesman for Quaker Oats. He sang a commercial with the praise "The giant of the cereals is Quaker Oats" and the cereal company sponsored Roy, his wife Dale, and his horse Trigger during several years of radio adventures.

Although they did not have any horses, other famous personalities who appeared in Quaker Oats commercials were Shirley Temple, Bing Crosby, Fred MacMurray, and Dick Powell.

Index

A

Allie-Oops, 100
Almonds
  Apricot-Filled Oatmeal Cookies,
    84–85
  Chocolate-Almond Delights, 40
  Jumbo Oat Cookies, 26
  Mocha Meringue Kisses, 70–71
  Oatmeal Cookies Caribbean, 133
Almost Instant Oatmeal Cookies, 137
Anzac Biscuits, 23
Apples
Apple Oatmeal Breakfast Cookies, 49
  Honey Apple Cookies, 135
  Oatmeal Snack Bars, 122–123
Applesauce
  Allie-Oops, 100
  Heart-Smart Oatmeal Cookies,
    72–73

Apricot
  Apricot-Filled Oatmeal Cookies,
    84–85
  Apricot-Oat Thumbprints, 58–59

B

Bacon, Breakfast Yum-Yums, 104
Baking cookies, tips for, 7–10
Banana liqueur, Fruit and Nut
  Goodness
  Cookies, 102
Bananas, Butterscotch Banana Drops,
  116
Bar cookies, method for, 8, 29
Bebe's No-Bakes, 127
Best-Ever Chip Chips, 75
Biscuits
  Anzac Biscuits, 23
  Oat Biscuits, 18

Blass, Bill, 15
Blueberry, Easy-Breezy Blueberry
    Treats, 66
Brandy, Dorothy's Brandied Oaties,
    90
Breakfast cookies
    Apple Oatmeal Breakfast Cookies,
        49
    Breakfast Yum-Yums, 104
Brownie Oat Cookies, 88
Butterscotch
    Best-Ever Chip Chips, 75
    Butterscotch Banana Drops,
        116
    Butterscotch No-Bakes, 64

C

Candied fruits
    Christmas Cookies, 114
    Heart-Smart Oatmeal Cookies,
        72–73
Caramel Oatmeal Bars, 82–83
Cha's "Got a Date With a Spicy Mac-
    Oatmeal Cookie," 94–95

Cheddar cheese, Breakfast Yum-
    Yums, 104
Chips in cookies, types of, 25
Choc-Oat-Chip Cookies, 28–29
Chocolate
    Allie-Oops, 100
    Best-Ever Chip Chips, 75
    Brownie Oat Cookies, 88
    Choc-Oat-Chip Cookies, 28–29
    Chocolate-Almond Delights, 40
    Chocolate Mint Dippers, 50–51
    Choco-Nut Chews, 108–109
    Delight Bites, 138
    melting method, 7
    Oat Drops, 106
    Oatmeal Chocolate Chippers, 78
    Oatmeal Cookies from Mars, 68
    Oregon Trail Bits, 129
    white
        Cranberry Chunk Cookies,
            80–81
        Oatmeal Plus-Plus Cookies,
            55
Choco-Nut Chews, 108–109
Christmas Cookies, 114

Cinnamon redhots, Heart-Smart
  Oatmeal Cookies, 72–73
Coconut
  Anzac Biscuits, 23
  Best-Ever Chip Chips, 75
  Cha's "Got A Date With a Spicy
    Mac-Oatmeal Cookie", 94–95
  Chocolate Mint Dippers, 50–51
  Coconut Crispies, 96
  Double-Decker Delights, 124–125
  Fruit and Nut Goodness Cookies,
    102
  Oatmeal Chocolate Chippers, 78
  Oatmeal Crisps, 19
  Peanut Butter Oatmeal Crunch
    Cookies, 76–77
  Yum Rum Cookies, 52
Coffee, Mocha Meringue Kisses,
  70–71
Commodore's Oatmeal Cookies, 98
Cookie sheets
  greased versus ungreased, 9
  recommended type, 8
Corn flakes, Commodore's Oatmeal
  Cookies, 98

Cranberry Chunk Cookies, 80–81
Cream Cheese Oatmeal Sandwiches,
  46–47

D

Dates
  Apple Oatmeal Breakfast Cookies,
    49
  Bebe's No-Bakes, 127
  Cha's "Got A Date With a Spicy
    Mac-Oatmeal Cookie", 94–95
  Date Filling, 119
  Fruit and Nut Goodness Cookies,
    102
  Heart-Smart Oatmeal Cookies,
    72–73
  J's Oatmeal Cookies, 131
  Oatkins, 110
  Oatmeal Trilbys, 118–119
  Penny's Pastries, 33
Decorating cookies, 10
Delight Bites, 138
Dorothy's Brandied Oaties, 90
Double-Decker Delights, 124–125
Drizzle topping, 59

E

Easy-Breezy Blueberry Treats, 66
English Matrimonials, 92

F

Figs, Heart-Smart Oatmeal Cookies,
    72–73
Filled cookies
    Apricot-Filled Oatmeal Cookies,
        84–85
    Cream Cheese Oatmeal
        Sandwiches, 46–47
    Double-Decker Delights, 124–125
    Oatmeal Trilbys, 118–119
    Rhubarb Oat Bars, 44–45
    Southern Oatmeal Bars, 42–43
Freezing cookies, 9
Frosted cookies
    Apricot-Oat Thumbprints, 58–59
    Caramel Oatmeal Bars, 82–83
    Chocolate Mint Dippers, 50–51
    Choco-Nut Chews, 108–109
    Frosted Orange Drops, 38–39

Frostings
    basic recipe, 39
    drizzle topping, 59
    Fudge Frosting, 109
    glaze recipe, 63
Fruit and Nut Goodness Cookies,
    102

G

Gerry's Molasses Cookies, 57
Glaze recipe, 63
Gum drops, Gum Drop Cookies, 37

H

Heart-Smart Oatmeal Cookies, 72–73
Honey Apple Cookies, 135

I

Icebox cookies, Oatmeal Icebox
    Cookies, 21

J

John McCann's Irish Oatmeal
Cookies, 30
J's Oatmeal Cookies, 131
Jumbo Oat Cookies, 26

K

Keating, Paul, 23

M

m & m's
Allie-Oops, 100
Oregon Trail Bits, 129
Macadamia nuts
Cha's "Got A Date With a Spicy
Mac-Oatmeal Cookie", 94–95
Fruit and Nut Goodness Cookies,
102
Oatmeal Plus-Plus Cookies, 55
McCann's Irish Oatmeal, John
McCann's Irish Oatmeal
Cookies, 30

Malted Oatmeal Bars, 120
Mint
Chocolate Mint Dippers, 50–51
Peppermint Toppers, 62–63
Mocha Meringue Kisses, 70–71
Molasses
Gerry's Molasses Cookies, 57
Heart-Smart Oatmeal Cookies,
72–73

N

Nantucket Bake Shop Oatmeal
Cookies, 32
Nicklaus, Jack and Barbara, 19
No-bake cookies
Almost Instant Oatmeal Cookies,
137
Bebe's No-Bakes, 127
Butterscotch No-Bakes, 64
Nuts
Butterscotch No-Bakes, 64
Caramel Oatmeal Bars, 82–83
Choc-Oat-Chip Cookies, 28

Nuts (*cont.*)
  Commodore's Oatmeal Cookies, 98
  Cream Cheese Oatmeal
    Sandwiches, 46–47
  J's Oatmeal Cookies, 131
  Oat Drops, 106
  Oatmeal Icebox Cookies, 21
  Rhubarb Oat Bars, 44–45
  Southern Oatmeal Bars, 42–43
  Yum Rum Cookies, 52
  See also recipes under specific types
    of nuts

O

Oat Biscuits, 18
Oat Drops, 106
Oatkins, 110
Oatmeal Chocolate Chippers, 78
Oatmeal Cookie Bites, 13
Oatmeal Cookies, basic recipes, 15,
    16, 24–25
Oatmeal Cookies Caribbean, 133
Oatmeal Cookies from Mars, 68
Oatmeal Crisps, 19
Oatmeal Icebox Cookies, 21

Oatmeal Plus-Plus Cookies, 55
Oatmeal Snack Bars, 122–123
Oatmeal Trilbys, 118–119
Orange-flavor, Frosted Orange
    Drops, 38
Oregon Trail Bits, 129
Oven thermometer, use of, 8

P

Peanut butter
  Allie-Oops, 100
  Bebe's No-Bakes, 127
  Cha's "Got a Date With a Spicy
    Mac-Oatmeal Cookie," 94–95
  Choco-Nut Chews, 108–109
  Delight Bites, 138
  Oat Drops, 106
  Peanut Butter Oatmeal Crunch
    Cookies, 76–77
Peanuts
  Choco-Nut Chews, 108–109
  Delight Bites, 138
  Peanut Butter Oatmeal Crunch
    Cookies, 76–77

Pecans
  Christmas Cookies, 114
  Cranberry Chunk Cookies, 80–81
  Double-Decker Delights, 124–125
  Oatmeal Chocolate Chippers, 78
  Oatmeal Cookies Caribbean, 133
  Oatmeal Cookies from Mars, 68
  Penny's Pastries, 33
  Peppermint Toppers, 62–63
  Pineapple, Fruit and Nut Goodness
    Cookies, 102
  Pumpkin, Oatkins, 110

Q

Quaker Oats recipes
  Choc-Oat-Chip Cookies, 28–29
  Jumbo Oat Cookies, 26
  Quaker's Best Oatmeal Cookies, 24
    basic recipe, 24
    nutritional information, 25
    variations, 25

R

Raisin bran cereal, Oregon Trail Bits,
  129

Raisin candies (chocolate-covered),
  Delight Bites, 138
Raisins
  Caramel Oatmeal Bars, 82–83
  Commodore's Oatmeal Cookies, 98
  Cream Cheese Oatmeal
    Sandwiches, 46–47
  Dorothy's Brandied Oaties, 90
  John McCann's Irish Oatmeal
    Cookies, 30
  J's Oatmeal Cookies, 131
  Nantucket Bake Shop Oatmeal
    Cookies, 32
  Oatkins, 110
  Oatmeal Cookies, 15
  Penny's Pastries, 33
  Rosy Rocks, 86
Raphael, Sally Jessy, 16
Raspberry jam, English
  Matrimonials, 92
Rhubarb Oat Bars, 44–45
Rice cereal
  Best-Ever Chip Chips, 75
  Peanut Butter Oatmeal Crunch
    Cookies, 76–77

Rosy Rocks, 86
Rum
    Oatmeal Cookies Caribbean, 133
    Yum Rum Cookies, 52

S

Sally's Oatmeal Cookies, 16
Scott, Willard, 13
Southern Oatmeal Bars, 42
Strawberry jam, English
    Matrimonials, 92
Substitutions in recipes, 7
Sweet potatoes, Southern Oatmeal
    Bars, 42–43

T

Tomato soup, Rosy Rocks, 86
Topped cookies, Oatmeal Snack
    Bars, 122–123
Toppings for cookies, 9
    Apple Topping, 123
    See also Frosted cookies; Frostings

V

Vanilla chips, Cranberry Chunk
    Cookies, 80–81

W

Walnuts
    Apple Oatmeal Breakfast Cookies,
        49
    Cranberry Chunk Cookies, 80–81
    Dorothy's Brandied Oaties, 90
    Gum Drop Cookies, 37
    John McCann's Irish Oatmeal
        Cookies, 30
    Malted Oatmeal Bars, 120
    Oatmeal Cookies, 15
    Oatmeal Cookies from Mars, 68
    Rosy Rocks, 86
Water chestnuts, Delight Bites, 138
Wheat germ, Breakfast Yum-Yums,
    104
White chocolate
    Cranberry Chunk Cookies, 80–81
    Oatmeal Plus-Plus Cookies, 55

Y

Yum Rum Cookies, 52

Z

Zucchini, Oatmeal Cookies from
Mars, 68